SHORTCUTS
for Guitar

Tips to make you a more
skillful player in no time

By Fred Sokolow

Edited by Ronny Schiff

Recording:
Guitar and vocals: Fred Sokolow
Sound Engineer: Michael Monagan
Recorded and mixed at Sossity Sound

PLAYBACK+
Speed • Pitch • Balance • Loop

To access audio visit:
www.halleonard.com/mylibrary

Enter Code
1118-6504-7884-2679

ISBN 978-1-4950-2178-7

7777 W. BLUEMOUND RD. P.O. BOX 13819 MILWAUKEE, WI 53213

In Australia Contact:
Hal Leonard Australia Pty. Ltd.
4 Lentara Court
Cheltenham, Victoria, 3192 Australia
Email: ausadmin@halleonard.com.au

Visit Hal Leonard Online at
www.halleonard.com

CONTENTS

INTRODUCTION

A student in one of my guitar classes said, "You keep showing us shortcuts that save time and make things easier. You ought to put them all in a book!" Here it is: a collection of tips that save time and energy and make you a more skillful player—in any musical genre.

The pros use shortcuts all the time. While transcribing the music of many great guitarists, I discovered that, if you find an easier way of playing a lick that, at first glance, seemed difficult, that's probably the way the pro was playing it!

Some of the shortcuts in this book will help your soloing; others make chord accompaniment easier, whether you're strumming or picking. Still other shortcuts will help you learn chord progressions more quickly and increase your understanding of music in general.

Speaking of "understanding of music," if any of the music theory lingo in the following pages goes over your head, there's a chapter on some music basics with helpful explanations for those who could use them.

The explanations of some of the shortcuts include audio examples. Be sure to listen to these soundclips, as an audio example is worth a thousand words!

Good luck,

SOME MUSIC BASICS

The following explanations may help you understand musical concepts that come up throughout this book.

Twelve Tones

There are twelve tones in Western music: A, A♯ (the same as B♭), B, C, C♯ (D♭), D, D♯ (E♭), E, F, F♯ (G♭), G, and G♯ (A♭).

➡ Sharp (♯) means "a fret higher"; flat (♭) means "a fret lower."

➡ Every sharp or flat note has two possible names; for example, F♯ is the same as G♭.

➡ There's no sharp or flat between B and C, or between E and F.

➡ There are several Cs, Ds, Es, etc. on the fretboard; for example, here are several C notes on the guitar:

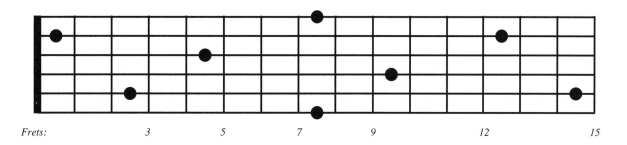

Frets: 3   5   7   9   12   15

The Major Scale

The major scale is the eight-note, "do-re-mi" scale that you've heard all your life. Chord construction and chord progressions are based on it, so it's good to understand how it works. The spacing of the notes defines the major scale's sound: all the notes are two frets apart, except the third and fourth notes and the seventh and eighth notes in the scale, which are one fret apart.

C Major Scale: C   D   E F   G   A   B C

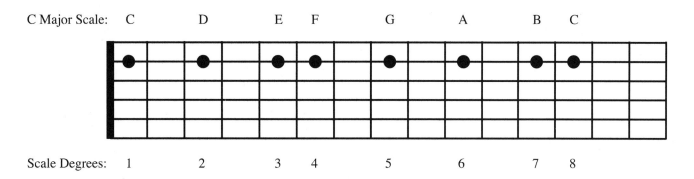

Scale Degrees: 1   2   3 4   5   6   7 8

➡ Every major scale has this same spacing.

➡ Notice that, in the C major scale above, the first and last notes are both C.

Keys

A key is like a tonal home base. If a song is in the key of C, it may or may not begin on a C chord, but it almost certainly *ends* on a C chord. When the song leaves the C chord and goes to any other chord, it causes tension. The tension is relieved, or *resolved*, when the song returns to the C chord. Strum the following four chords, four strums per measure, over and over and you'll hear how the tune sounds unfinished when you end on any chord but C:

Chords

A chord is three or more notes played simultaneously. The distance (interval) between the notes determines the type of chord:

➡ A *major chord* is constructed from the first, third, and fifth notes of its major scale. For example, a C major chord (often just called a C chord) consists of the first, third, and fifth notes of the C major scale: C, E, and G. Major chords sound sunny and complete.

➡ A *minor chord* has a different interval formula: 1–♭3–5. It's the same as a major chord, but the 3rd is flatted (lowered) one fret. Minor chords may sound melancholy.

➡ A seventh chord has four notes: 1–3–5–♭7. It's the same as a major chord but with one note added: the ♭7th. Seventh chords sound bluesy and create tension.

➡ There are other chord types, but most of them are variations of these three types: major, minor, and seventh.

The Numbers System

The language of music is often expressed with numbers rather than letters. Musicians say, "Go to the IV chord," or "Go to the II minor." The numbers refer to the major scale. Since C is the first note in the C major scale, a C chord is the I chord in the key of C. D (or D7 or Dm) is the II chord; E is the III chord, and so on. In the key of D, E is the II chord.

No matter which key you're in, going from the I chord to the V chord has a certain sound. So does going from I to IV. It's the spaces between chords—the *intervals*—that give a chord progression its unique sound. Once you can recognize the sounds of the various intervals (I to IV, ii [minor] to V), you understand how music works and you can play a song in any key. You're not just memorizing letter names; you're feeling the song's structure.

The I–IV–V Chord Family

Regardless of a song's key, the I, IV, and V chords are the "usual suspects"—the chords that are most likely to occur. Millions of folk, country, blues, bluegrass, and classic rock songs consist of just those three chords. They can be in any order imaginable. It's helpful to have the chord families memorized: I, IV, and V = C, F, and G in the key of C, for example.

SOLOING SHORTCUTS

Soloing involves strategies. When you hear a guitarist *shredding*—his fingers flying over the fretboard—he's not flying blind; he's working a system, perhaps combining a few systems. He may be basing his solo on a scale with which he's become comfortable, or his licks may be based on chord shapes. Either way, his solo, whether memorized or ad-libbed, is based on a strategy. Chances are, one of the following shortcuts is at play.

SHORTCUT #1: The Blues Box

This is the most popular shortcut of all, especially among beginning rock and blues guitarists. Often, it's the only soloing strategy they know. The blues box allows you to:

➡ Ad-lib blues or rock solos

➡ Stay in one position on the fretboard, even though a song has many chord changes

➡ Ad-lib solos to songs in a minor key

➡ Ad-lib solos to any "bluesy" song, regardless of genre (country, rockabilly, jazz, bluegrass, rock, blues, etc.). A song is "bluesy" if the singer is singing blue notes (♭3rds and ♭7ths)

➡ Play the melody of many bluesy songs

It's called a "box" because the pattern it makes on the fretboard is somewhat box-shaped.

The more "musically correct" name for the blues box is the "minor pentatonic scale." Pentatonic means "five-note," and the scale is minor because it includes a ♭3rd and ♭7th. However, to make use of the blues box, you don't need to know what any of that means! Here it is in the key of F, written as a loop that you can repeat over and over in order to get it into your fingers. It goes up, then comes back down. Place your index finger on the sixth string, first fret and play it!

Blues Box in F

1

> **Technical note for music theory wonks**
> When playing the above scale, you may notice that it contains more than five notes. After the fifth note (fourth string, first fret), you're starting over, just an octave higher (fourth string, third fret). After the fifth note in that register, you start over again (first string, first fret), but the box only contains the first two notes of that octave.

How to Use the Blues Box

A scale is like an alphabet (with notes instead of letters). You use the letters in the alphabet to make words, and you use the notes in a scale to make musical licks and phrases, like these:

Blues Box Licks

Using these and similar phrases, here's an example of an ad-libbed solo to a blues tune. It's in the key of F:

12-Bar Blues in F

Notice that the blues licks you generate from the blues box work *over the chord changes*; you don't have to change positions with each chord change! Also, notice that very simple licks can drive a good-sounding solo. Interesting *timing* makes it work.

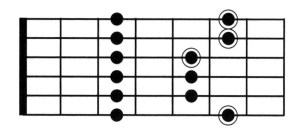

Bending strings
It really starts to sound bluesy when you bend strings (this is also called *stretching* or *choking* strings). The circled notes in the following diagram show which notes can be bent. Some bends raise the string's pitch one fret; some raise the pitch two frets.

Here's a solo with some string bending added to the mix:

Blues-Rock in A

What makes the blues box such a great shortcut is:

➡ While the song's chords are changing, you can stay in the blues box, and the licks you make up will work with all the chords in the tune.

➡ If you stick to the notes in the box, then you almost can't hit a wrong note.

➡ Since it doesn't include any open strings, it's moveable, so you can use it to play in any key.

A Minor Pentatonic

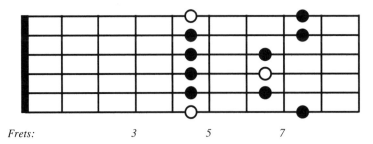

Frets: 3   5   7

The blues box works as a soloing strategy for songs in a minor key. Here's a rock progression in A minor. The solo is built from the A blues box:

Blues-Rock in A Minor

  5

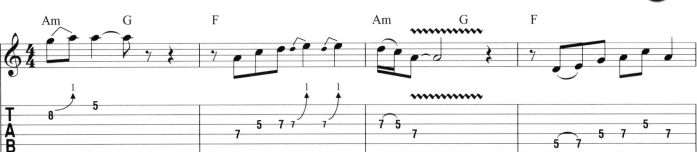

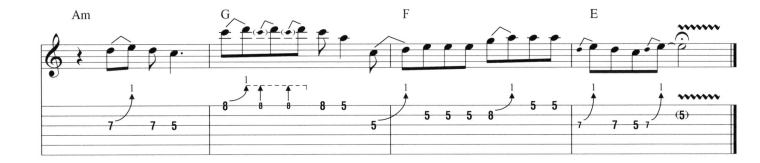

NOTE: The blues box is a springboard for ad-libbed solos, but often it can be used to play a bluesy song's melody, as well.

Once you become adept at using the blues box to create musical licks and phrases, it's a valuable, versatile tool. You can acquire this skill by learning bluesy solos and by listening to (and playing along with) recordings of great blues and rock guitarists. It's like learning a language—listen to those who speak it well and then imitate their licks and phrases.

SHORTCUT #2: Using the Blues Box on Non-Bluesy Tunes

This shortcut makes the blues box usable in almost any tune, even if it doesn't fit the aforementioned descriptions. If you try the blues box soloing strategy on a song and it clashes or sounds inappropriate, *move it down three frets.*

For example, try blues-box-based solos on this rock ballad progression. It's in the key of C, so play the box at the eighth fret.

Chilly Winds Progression

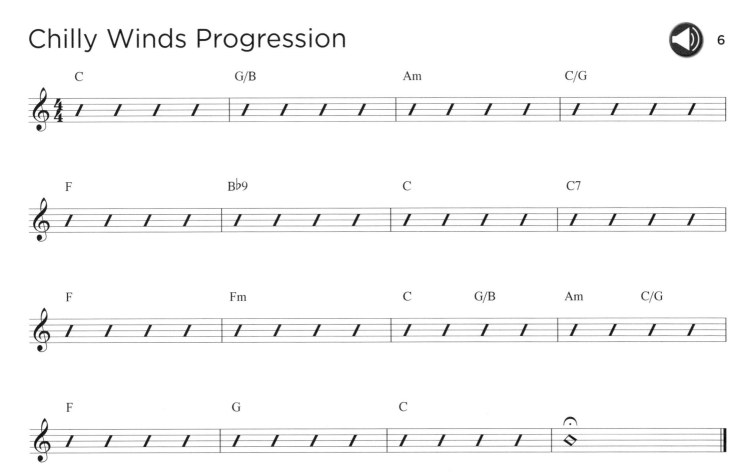

If you tried to solo as suggested, the result was probably not very musical; in fact, your licks probably clashed with the chord progression. Some songs don't lend themselves to blues-box soloing. When the blues box sounds wrong, move it down three frets (in this case, from the eighth fret to the fifth fret) and try it that way.

Chilly Winds Solo

The long explanation for *why* this works involves the concept of *relative minors*: Every major chord has a closely-related *relative minor* chord built on the 6th interval of the major scale. For example, *the sixth note in the C major scale is A, so Am is the relative minor of C.* If you play first-position C and Am chords, you can see how similar they are—they share several notes. They also share *scales.* The A minor scale has the same notes as the C major scale. That's why the A minor pentatonic solo above works for a tune in the key of C major.

Did the above paragraph sail right over your head? Then just remember: *When the blues box doesn't sound right with a song, move it down three frets!*

Summing Up

The "blues box moved down three frets" strategy means that you can use the minor pentatonic scale to solo over almost any tune. On bluesy or minor-key songs, use it in the actual key (e.g., in the key of C, play at the eighth fret, where the sixth string is a C note). On songs where the box sounds "off," move it down three frets, to the relative-minor key.

SHORTCUT #3: Sliding Major Pentatonics

The "sliding major pentatonic scales" are extremely useful in rock and country soloing. They work well on tunes in which the blues box sounds inappropriate. These scales span nine or 10 frets, so they offer a wide range of sounds, from the lower to the higher register.

Like the blues box, these are pentatonic (five-note) scales, but they include only major-scale notes (1–2–3–5–6). Play the two scales below over and over, ascending and descending the fretboard. Be sure to use the indicated fingering and slides. The first five notes of each scale may remind you of the hook to the classic pop/R&B song "My Girl."

F Major Pentatonic Scale (Sixth-string Root)

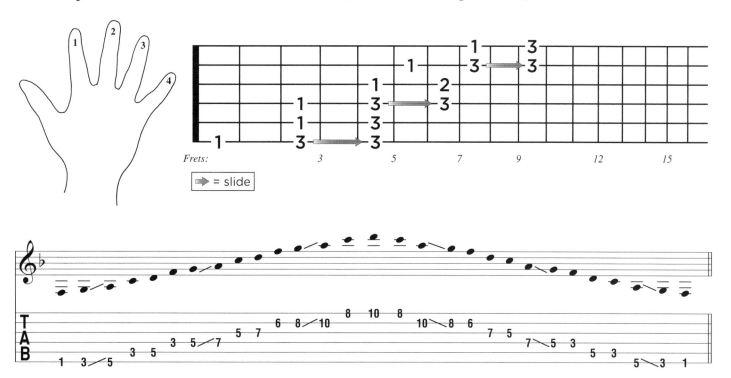

Bb Major Pentatonic Scale (Fifth-string Root)

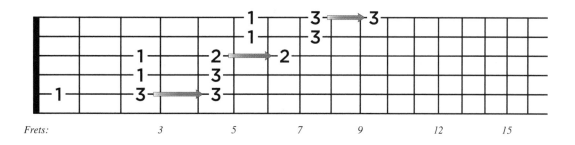

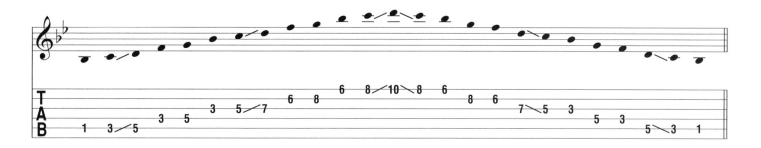

Like the blues box, you usually don't have to change scales with the chord changes of a tune. However, unlike blues-box soloing, you may have to change scales when a tune stays on a chord for several bars. If a song in the key of C goes to G and stays on the G chord for four or more bars, it may sound better to switch to a G major pentatonic scale for those bars.

Here's a country-rock progression in the key of G. The first half of the solo is based on the sixth-string-root pentatonic scale, and the second half on the fifth-string-root scale. The chords change quickly enough that you can base all your soloing on the G major pentatonic scale.

Country-Rock Progression
8

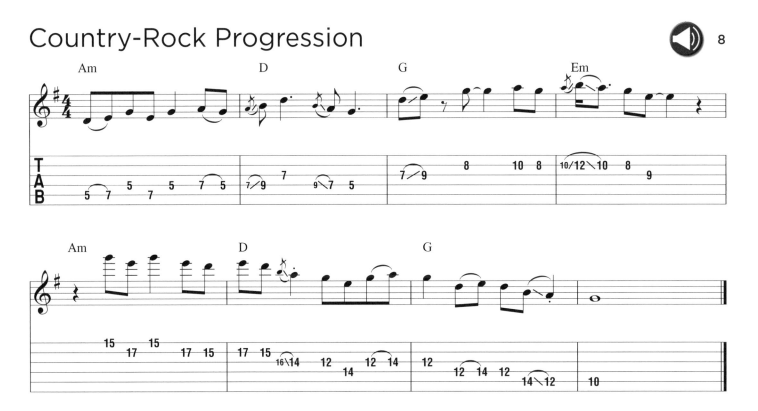

Southern Rock in C
9

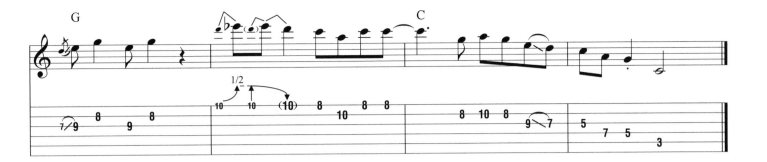

Here's one more sample tune. This one is in the style of the Allman Brothers' Dickey Betts, who often used major pentatonic sliding scales as the basis for his solos. The song is in the key of A, but it stays on the E chord for several bars, so the soloist switches to the E major pentatonic scale for that part of the tune.

Place Your Betts

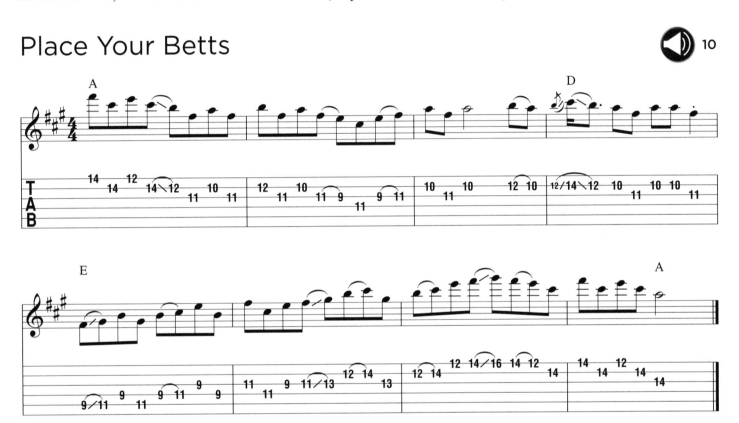

Summing Up

Countless classic rock and country solos are based on the major pentatonic sliding scales. Once you know how to use them, they are as versatile as the blues box. Some tunes to listen to that are textbook examples of the use of this strategy include the Allman Brothers' "Ramblin' Man," the Beatles' "Let It Be" (George Harrison's solos), and Rod Stewart's "Maggie May" (Ron Wood's solos).

SHORTCUT #4: Moving the F Formation Around

The *F formation* is the basis for many famous solos in blues, jazz, rock, country, and most genres you can name. It's the abbreviated version of the barred F chord, so it has a first-string root, and that's how you place it on the fretboard. You can play a two-finger or three-finger version of it:

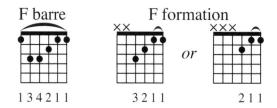

➡ You can base solos on the notes of the F formation, playing chords or arpeggios (picking out individual notes, going up and down the chord) and moving the formation around to match the chords in a song:

Arpeggios

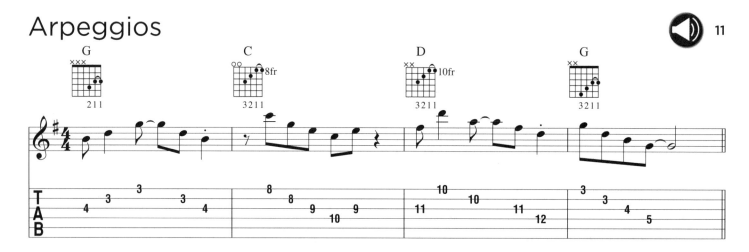

➡ You can make solos and licks more interesting by adding major-scale notes that are adjacent to the F formation (the hollow circles are adjacent major-scale notes).

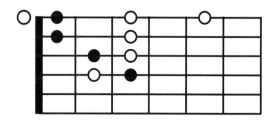

Country Swing

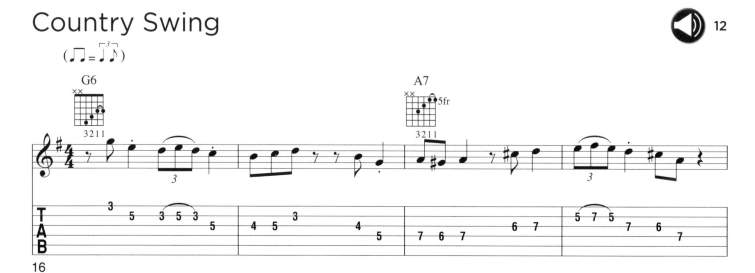

16

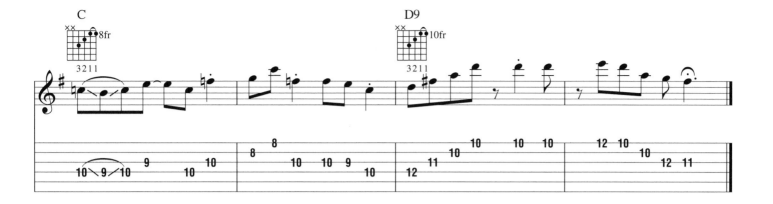

➡ Add some blue notes (♭3rd, ♭7th, and ♭5th) to add more flavor to your solos:

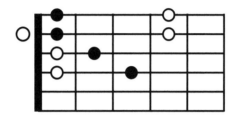

Country Swing #2

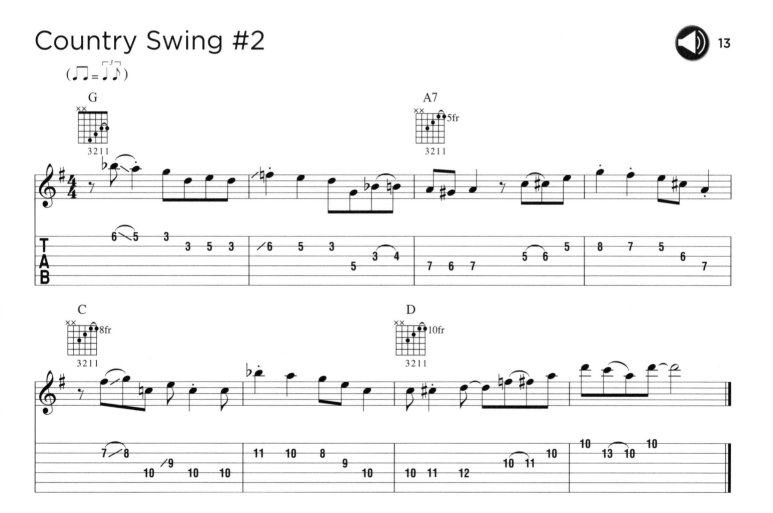

Summing Up

Once you start using the F formation to invent licks and solos, you'll hear it in the playing of your favorite guitarists, whatever the genre.

SHORTCUT #5: Steve Cropper Licks— Another F Formation-based Strategy

Steve Cropper played his Telecaster with Booker T and the MGs, a band that had several instrumental hits and backed up all the Stax/Volt artists, such as Otis Redding and Sam and Dave. One strategy that he often employed involved a set of licks on the first and third strings that emanate from the F formation. Many iconic R&B licks were based on it, but it's also heard in country music, folk-rock, and blues.

As shown below, play the first and third strings simultaneously while playing an F formation. You can pick them with the thumb and index finger, or with a flatpick and the middle finger.

Steve Cropper Lick

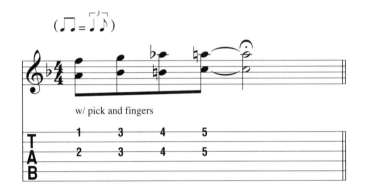

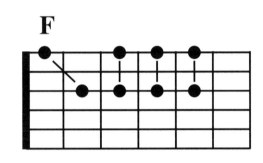

You can vary these licks by playing the first and third strings separately and by starting at the high end of the lick (rather than starting at the F formation). You can also leave out some of the components:

Variations

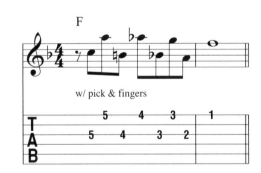

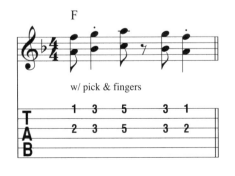

Once you've got these ideas down, you can follow a tune's chords around, playing F formations and executing the above licks. Often, a lead guitarist will use this bag of tricks to play fills and backup licks behind a singer. For example, here's a blues/rock progression that lends itself to this strategy. It's a three-chord, 12-bar blues in D, so your licks are based on these three F formations:

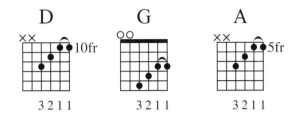

Stagolee

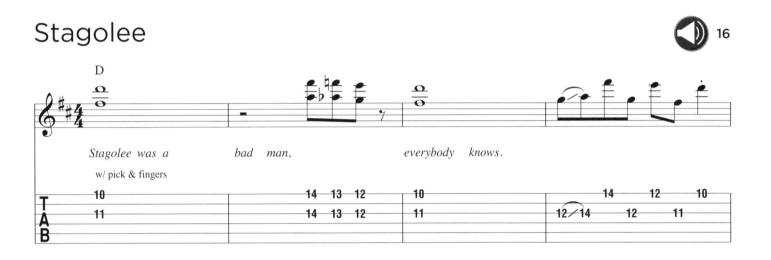

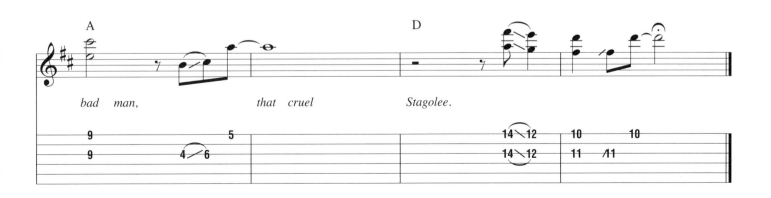

Here's a brief R&B solo built on the same ideas:

R&B Solo in D

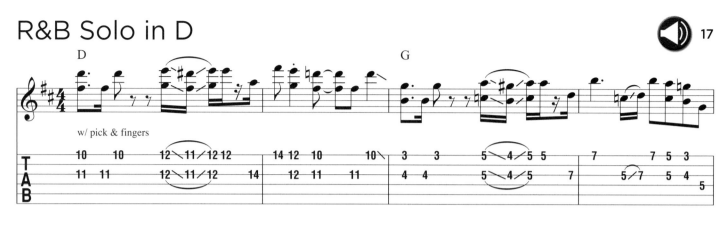

To expand this concept, you can play two-finger, partial seventh and ninth chords that are based on the F formation. You go higher for the seventh chord and lower for the ninth chord:

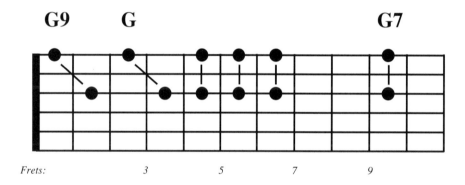

The ninth chord is just a fancier seventh chord, and both chords usually lead "up a 4th" (e.g., D7 leads to G, and A7 makes you want to hear a D chord). Listen to Track 18 and play the solo, "Seven to Nine"; it shows how to make use of the seventh and ninth chord extensions:

Seven to Nine

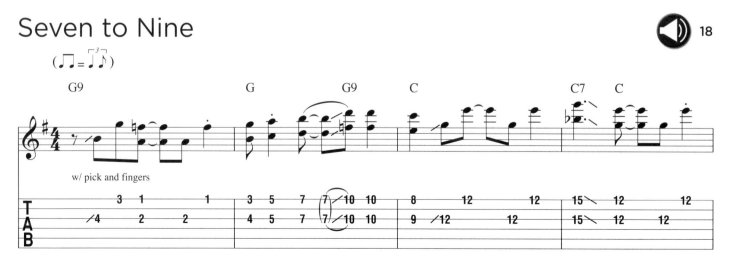

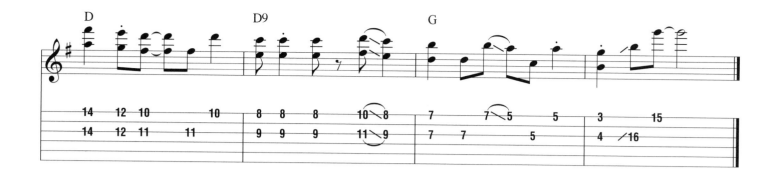

Summing Up

These first-and-third-string licks are an easy lead guitar technique—*if* you are quick at finding F formation versions of chords. Remember: the first string is the root of the F formation, so that's how you place a chord; for example, the first string, fifth fret is an A note, so if you play the F formation at the fifth fret of the first string, you'll get an A chord.

For some classic examples of this strategy in action, listen to Bob Dylan's "She Belongs to Me" or Sam and Dave's "Soul Man."

SHORTCUT #6: Soloing off the F formation/I Chord

If a song stays in the immediate chord family (I, IV, and V and the relative minors of I, IV, and V), you don't have to move the F formations around to match the song's chord changes; you can stay on the I chord throughout. Here are a few examples:

Rhythm Changes

 19

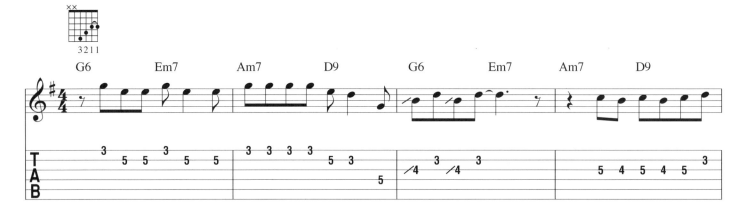

Rock Ballad in C

 20

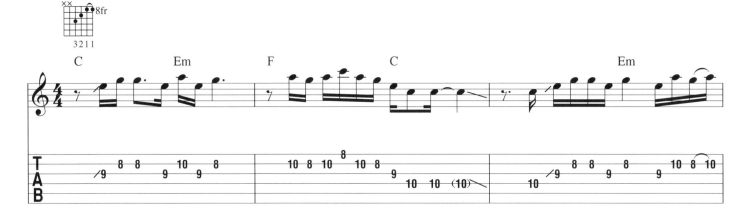

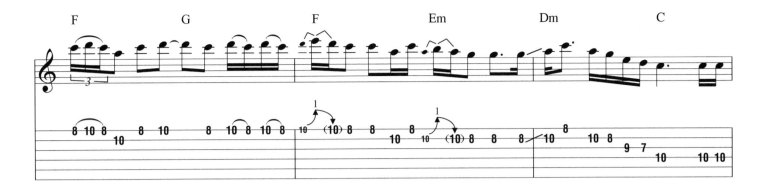

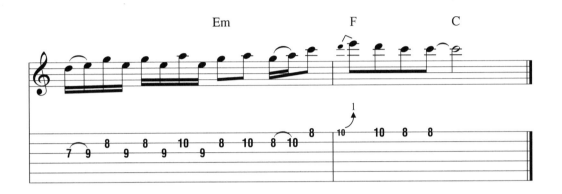

Summing Up

It's amazing how well this simple strategy works on a variety of types of music, especially once you become familiar enough with the adjacent major scale and blue notes and can use them to build coherant solos.

SHORTCUT #7: Soloing off the Ninth-Chord Shape

Some chord shapes lend themselves to easy-to-play guitar licks. When the fifth-string-root ninth chord appears in a tune, you can play the notes in the three-fret box shown below:

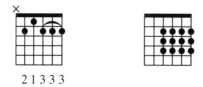

2 1 3 3 3

Here are some sample licks. Some are single-note phrases; others involve pairs of notes or three notes at once:

Ninth Chord Licks

21

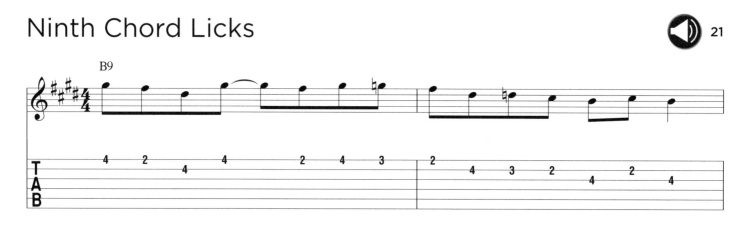

A much-used eight-bar bridge, sometimes called the "I Got Rhythm" bridge, will be discussed in another section of this book. In the key of G, the bridge looks like this:

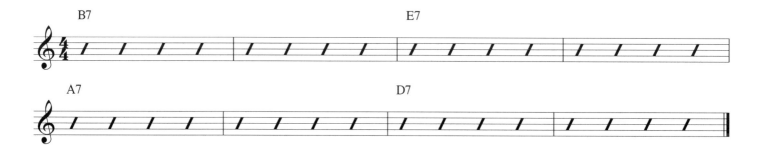

Ninth chords are just seventh chords with one extra note. You can usually substitute one for the other and it changes the color of the progression just slightly. So, the soloist can conceive of the "I Got Rhythm" bridge in the following way and ad-lib solos like the one below, which combines ninth-chord licks and F-formation licks:

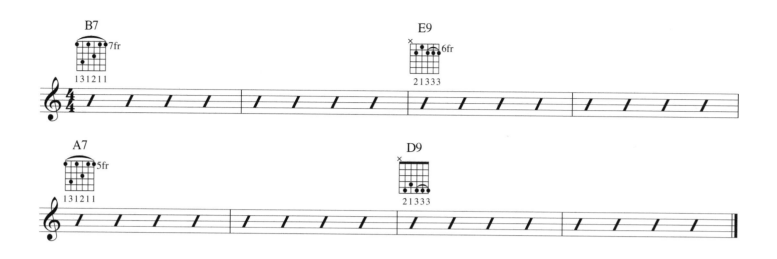

"I Got Rhythm" Bridge – Rock

22

Here's a jazzy version of the same bridge:

"I Got Rhythm" Bridge – Swing

The same strategy can be used in any key. Below is a solo to an R&B progression. The soloist is using F formation and ninth-chord formation licks:

R&B Interlude

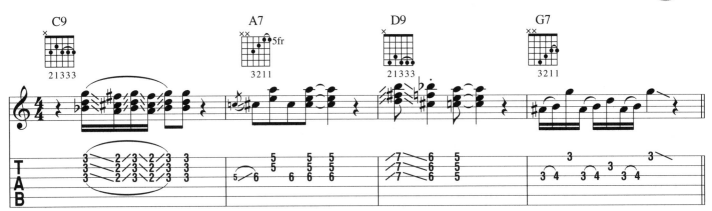

Summing Up

If you combine the ninth-chord formation licks with F-formation licks, you can create chord-based solos for tunes that go well beyond the standard I–IV–V changes.

SHORTCUT #8: Soloing off Two Minor-Chord Shapes

If you want to base your solos on chords, the F formation and ninth-chord formation are platforms for ad-libbed licks and solos. But if a song includes a minor chord, or a few minor chords, you'll need some minor formations and licks associated with them. Here are two handy minor chord forms:

Here's an example of a lead guitar playing arpeggios based on these minor chord shapes, as well the F and ninth-chord formations:

Minor Chord Shape Licks

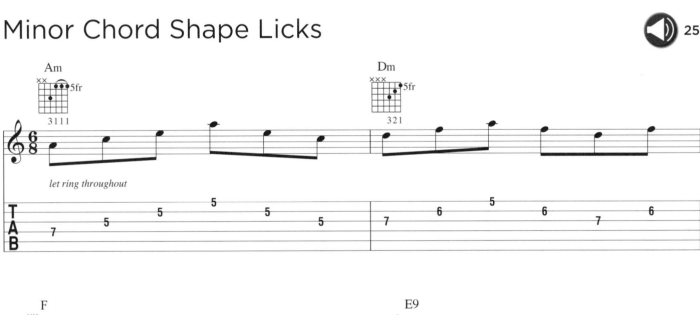

There are useful "other notes" (mostly minor scale tones) surrounding each of these moveable chord shapes:

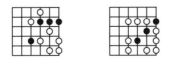

The solo to the following minor-key swing progression shows how to build licks and phrases from these minor shapes, playing both arpeggios and useful adjacent notes:

Minor Swingology

 26

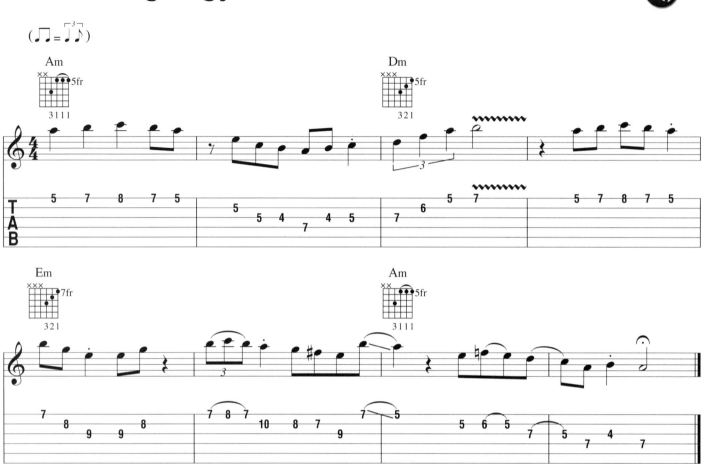

Here's a rock solo based on the same strategy:

Three Minors

 27

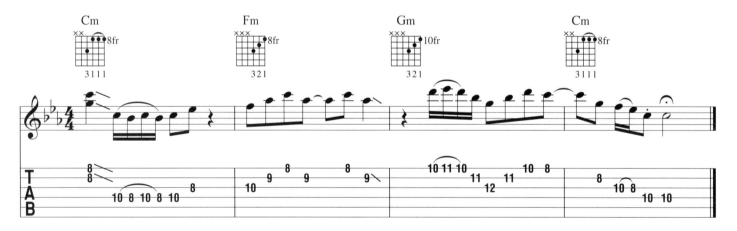

Summing Up

Once you can play solos based on minor shapes, the ninth-chord formation, and the F formation, you can cover almost any chord progression.

SHORTCUT #9: Soloing off Two More Major-Chord Shapes

To further expand your chord-based soloing, you need two more moveable major chord shapes and the useful notes that surround them:

The D Shape and the A Shape

Here are some licks you can build from the D shape and the A shape:

D-shape and A-shape Licks

28

The following R&B solo is built on the above ideas. It's reminiscent of the style of Curtis Mayfield and other early-'60s guitarists who influenced Jimi Hendrix (think "Little Wing" or "The Wind Cries Mary") and many other rock and R&B guitarists:

Little Mary

29

These major-chord positions can be just as useful in bluegrass, as the following solo shows:

Wreck of Old 97

30

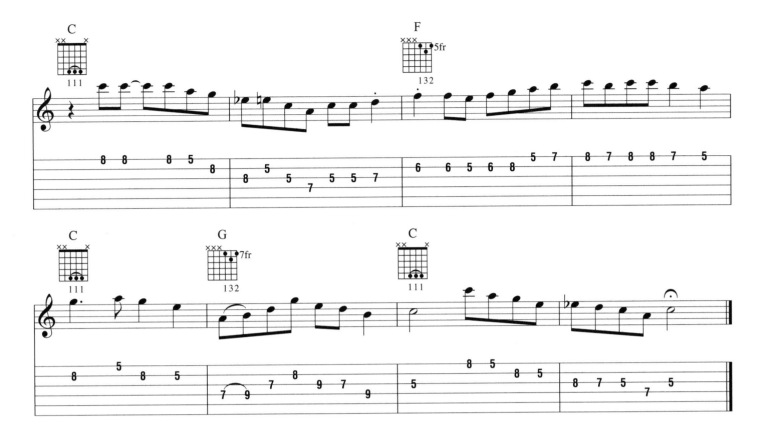

Summing Up

With all of these moveable chord shapes and the licks and solos they can generate, you can be a truly versatile, chord-based soloist.

RHYTHM GUITAR SHORTCUTS

The standard 12-bar blues progression is the basis for thousands of songs, so if you understand how that sequence of chords works, you can automatically play all the 12-bar tunes, in any key! There are other standard progressions that are the basis for many tunes, or parts of tunes, and familiarity with any of these patterns is a shortcut to learning many songs.

There are visual patterns on the fretboard that can help you locate chords or play chord progressions. These are also useful shortcuts.

SHORTCUT #10: Power Chords

In blues, rock, and sometimes modern country, rhythm guitarists play two-finger "power chords" instead of full five- or six-string chords. They're easy to play (especially when compared to barre chords) and they have a rhythmic, driving sound.

Power chords are the bottom two notes of barre chords. *They are shortcuts to playing barre chords!* For example:

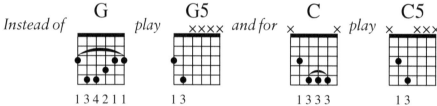

The power chords have a "5" in their name because they are incomplete chords that contain only the root and the 5th. A full major chord has three notes: the root, 3rd, and 5th. The 3rd is missing from power chords. (If that info is meaningless to you, please see the "Some Music Basics" chapter at the beginning of this book.

Here's an example of a basic rock progression along the lines of "Louie Louie," "Wild Thing," or "Twist and Shout," played with power chords in the key of A:

Powerchordia
🔊 31

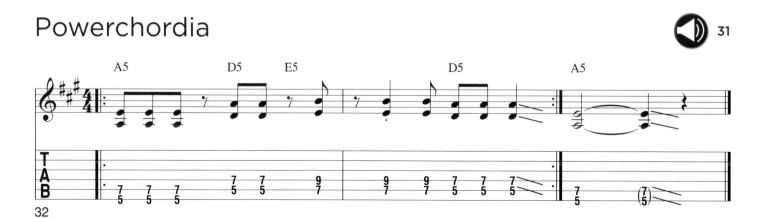

32

➡ Boogie backup patterns are often created from power chords. To play them, you have to stretch the pinky of your chording hand, as shown in the exercise below:

Boogieville

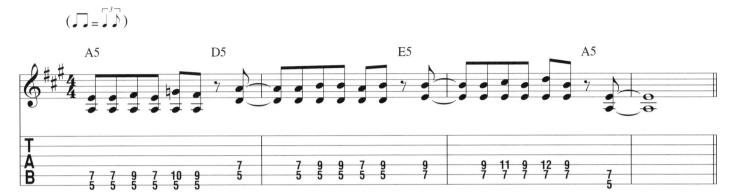

➡ Since power chords contain no 3rd, you can't tell if they're major or minor. This is fitting, as they are often used in bluesy tunes, and the blues is often ambiguous and contains both major and minor scale notes. So, you can use power chords in place of barred minor chords:

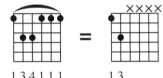

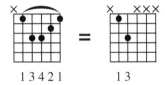

Summing Up

Power chords are easier to play than their barred counterparts, and they provide a strong rhythmic pulse. They lend themselves to bluesy songs, and it's easy to build boogie bass patterns around them.

SHORTCUT #11: Power-Chord Chord Families

When you learn about chord families and how they're played using power chords, you can automatically play countless tunes in any key with very little forethought.

Millions of tunes consist of just three chords: the I ("one") chord, IV ("four") chord, and V ("five") chord. The numbers refer to the major scale steps of whatever key you're in. For example, in the key of C, C is the I chord (because C is the first note in the C major scale); F is the IV chord (F is the fourth note in the C major scale); and G is the V chord (G is the fifth note in the C major scale). The I, IV, and V chords, in any key, constitute a "chord family."

There are countless three-chord songs in blues, classic rock, pop, country, folk, and bluegrass built on the chord family. If you use power chords to play them, they configure like this:

"Powerchordia" (Track 31) is a typical example of this I–IV–V configuration in the key of A, starting with a I chord that has a sixth-string root. You could also play it in the key of D, using the fifth-string-root I-chord configuration:

Powerchordia (with a fifth-string-root I chord) 🔊 33

34

➡ The chord-family configurations are moveable. If you use them, there are no "difficult keys." Playing in E♭, A♭, or any other "guitar unfriendly" key is just the same as playing in E or A. For example:

Family Ties

Key of D:

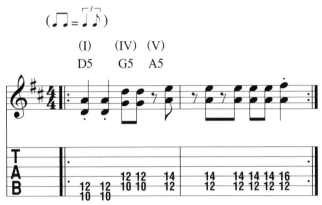

Key of D♭:

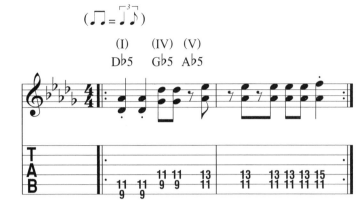

Key of D:

Key of D♭:

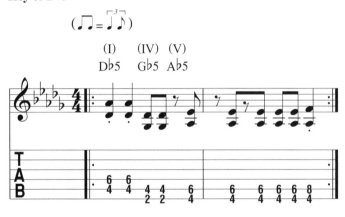

➡ You can play these chord-family configurations with complete barre chords instead of power chords. For instance:

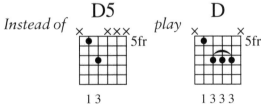

Summing up

Once you understand the I–IV–V power chord family configurations, it becomes easy to play simple tunes in any key, on two different places on the fretboard. You don't have to stop and think, "Where's the IV chord?" Or "Where's the V chord?" Because their placement on the fretboard is automatic in relation to the I chord.

SHORTCUT #12: Barre Chords: A Shortcut to Increasing Chord Vocabulary

Barre chords are difficult for many beginners. It takes a certain amount of strength to play them and a lot of repetition before they become familiar and comfortable. Here's the good news: If you learn just one barre-chord shape, you can play almost any chord by moving that shape around the fretboard and, in some cases, altering it slightly by lifting one finger!

Here's the shape. It's a major chord with a sixth-string root (the chord gets its name from the sixth-string note):

F

1 3 4 2 1 1

➡ If you know the notes on the sixth string (see Shortcut #20), you can move this shape around to play any major chord:

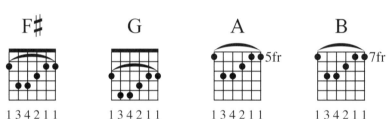

F♯   G   A   B
1 3 4 2 1 1   1 3 4 2 1 1   1 3 4 2 1 1   1 3 4 2 1 1

➡ If you play the barred major chord and lift your index finger from the third string, it becomes a minor chord:

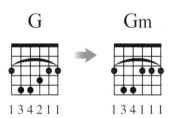

G   Gm
1 3 4 2 1 1   1 3 4 1 1 1

➡ The minor barre chord has the same root note (the sixth string), so you place it on the fretboard just as you placed the major chord:

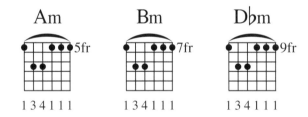

Am   Bm   D♭m
1 3 4 1 1 1   1 3 4 1 1 1   1 3 4 1 1 1

➡ If you play the major barre chord and lift your pinky finger from the fourth string, it becomes a seventh chord:

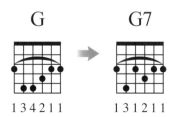

G   G7
1 3 4 2 1 1   1 3 1 2 1 1

You can play countless tunes using this one barre-chord shape, moving it around the fretboard. For example, here's "House of the Rising Sun" in the key of Fm, using only sixth-string-root barre chords:

House of the Rising Sun

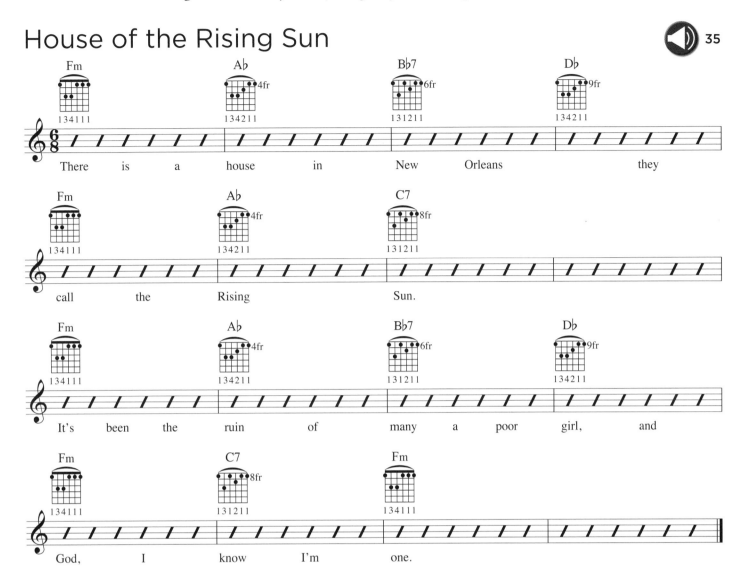

The same process applies to the fifth-string-root barre chord:

With a slight change, the major chord becomes minor or dominant (seventh), and you can play it on the fretboard by finding the appropriate note on the fifth string:

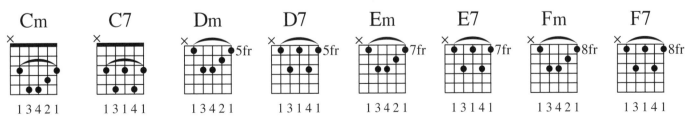

Summing Up

By learning just two barred major chord shapes, and knowing how to alter them to turn them into sevenths or minor chords, you can greatly increase your chord vocabulary.

SHORTCUT #13: The 12-Bar Blues Form

The 12-bar blues form is not just found in blues tunes; it's in early rock, rockabilly, country, bluegrass, swing, bebop, and even Broadway show tunes. Early rock and R&B songs like "Hound Dog," "Tutti Frutti," "Whole Lotta Shakin' Goin' On," "Johnny B. Goode," and "Shake, Rattle and Roll" are 12-bar blues tunes. So are "Kansas Ciy," "Folsom Prison Blues," and "Route 66."

Written music is divided into *bars*, or *measures*, each of which consists of a certain number of beats. For example, most rock tunes are in 4/4 time, and each bar contains four beats. When you see a drummer start a tune by clicking his drumsticks together over his head while counting to four, he's counting out one bar of music. This tells the band how fast the tune is (i.e., the tempo) and enables them to start together on the first beat of the next bar.

Most popular music is written in multiples of eight bars. Typically, there are eight-, 16-, or 32-bar phrases. So, the 12-bar blues is a unique form (it doesn't consist of eight-bar phrases). Like the blues scale, it may have come from Africa.

The 12-bar blues progression is best described using numbers, rather than letters. If the expressions "one chord," "four chord," and "five chord" are still a little hazy, go to the section on "The Numbers System" in the "Some Music Basics" chapter before continuing.

In its most basic form, the 12-bar blues consists of three four-bar phrases, as in "Woke Up This Morning," which follows:

Woke Up This Morning

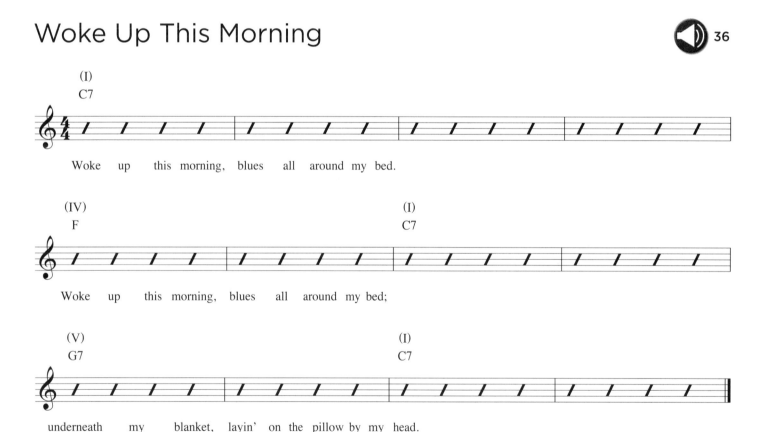

> ➡ Notice that the first two four-bar phrases have the same lyrics, and the third phrase rhymes with them. Most 12-bar blues tunes do this.

> ➡ As you can see, the three phrases are:
>   • The "I-chord phrase": four bars of the I chord
>   • The "IV-chord phrase": two bars of the IV chord and two bars of the I chord
>   • The "V chord phrase": two bars of the V chord and two bars of the I chord

- There are some common variations of this formula. The most frequent ones are:
  - In the first phrase, the second bar is the IV chord.
  - In the third phrase, the second bar is the IV chord.
  - In the third phrase, the last two bars contain a "turnaround"—a two-bar series of chords that signals the end of the progression and usually leads to another verse. It can be I–V or I–IV–I–V or other similar variations.
- Here's a verse to "Woke Up This Morning" that contains these variations:

Woke Up This Morning (with variations)

37

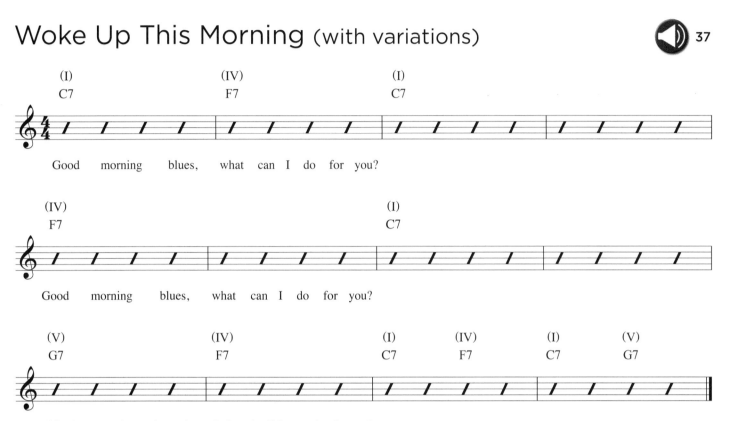

- Notice all the seventh chords (C7, F7, and G7). In many blues tunes, seventh chords are used throughout instead of major chords.
- You can alter the Power-Chord Chord Families info (Shortcut #11) slightly to get a shortcut to playing electric blues backup in any key. Instead of playing the complete barre chords, play bluesy seventh and ninth chords, like this:

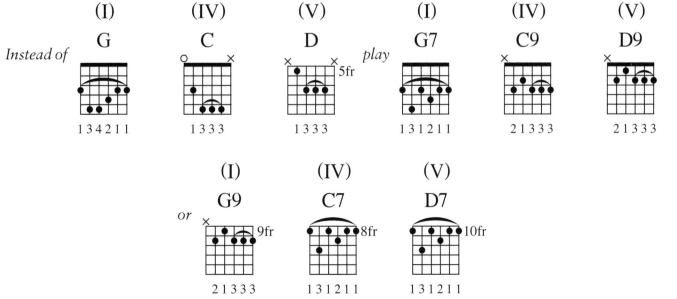

In case you're wondering, a ninth chord is just a fancier seventh chord; it's a seventh chord with one extra note: the 9th.

To illustrate the use of these altered, moveable chord families, here's an instrumental version of "Woke Up This Morning" played twice around the 12 bars; first, in the key of A, then in the key of D.

Woke Up This Morning (with moveable blues chords) 38

Key of A:

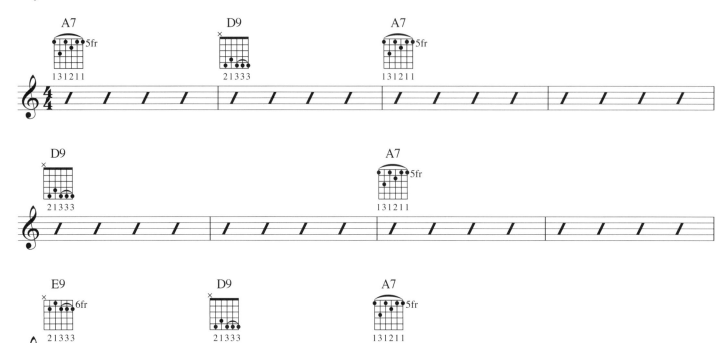

Key of D:

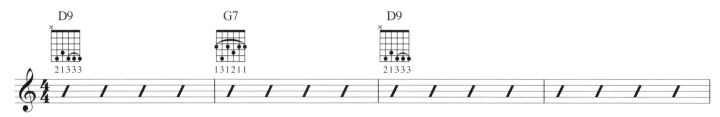

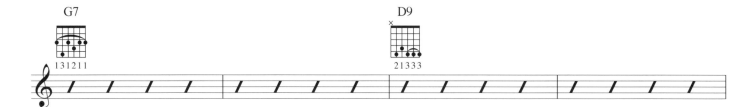

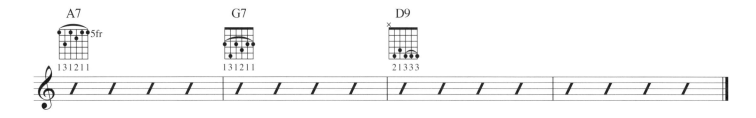

Summing up

Once you've played the 12-bar blues exercises, above, you'll start recognizing this progression whenever you hear it. It'll make it easier to learn countless tunes and play backup to them in any key using power chords or fuller blues chords.

SHORTCUT #14: The 8-Bar Blues Form

Many well-known blues tunes have an eight-bar progression, including "Key to the Highway," "How Long Blues," "Sittin' on Top of the World," "Come Back Baby," When Things Go Wrong with You (It Hurts Me Too)," and "Trouble in Mind."

Here's the basic chord pattern as well as a common variation.

As in "How Long Blues," "Come Back Baby," and "When Things Go Wrong with You (It Hurts Me Too)":

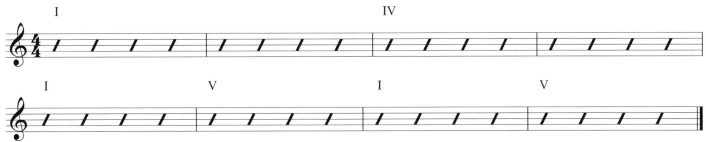

As in "Key to the Highway" and "Trouble in Mind":

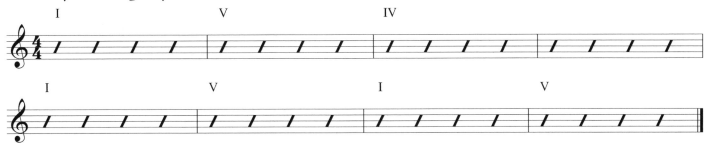

Here's a sample 8-bar blues that uses the second pattern, with a V chord in the second bar:

Didn't See It Coming

I was blind, I was sleeping, I was walkin' around in a daze,

I didn't see it comin', I couldn't see her goin' away.

➡ Just as with 12-bar blues tunes, many 8-bar blues songs have slight variations of the basic pattern. Listen to different versions of the songs mentioned above and see if you can map out their progressions, using numbers instead of letters.

Summing up
Like the 12-bar blues, the 8-bar pattern becomes familiar once you play several tunes of this type. You'll recognize other 8-bar blues when you hear them, and you'll be able to play them in any key by applying the above info on chord families and moveable blues chords.

SHORTCUT #15: Turnarounds

Most blues tunes and many popular songs have turnarounds—brief musical phrases at the end of a progression. They are often the last two bars of a 12-bar or 8-bar blues, but they are also used in standards from the '20s, '30s, and '40s. Once you know a few standard turnarounds, you know the last two bars to thousands of songs.

> **Blues Turnarounds**
> Here are some often-used blues turnarounds that end an 8-bar or 12-bar blues. Sometimes they're used as an intro (to begin a song), as well:

Blues Turnarounds

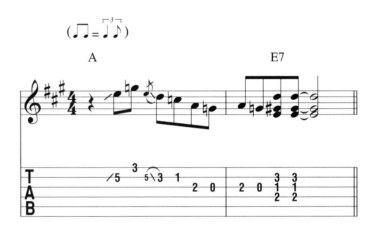

Turnarounds can be expressed in *numbers*, like this:

So, in the key of C, you'd get:

Lowercase Roman numerals mean "minor." So, "iv" is a "four minor" chord.

Here are some moveable turnarounds (they don't make use of open strings, so they can be played all over the fretboard, in any key):

Moveable Blues Turnarounds

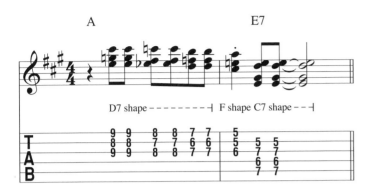

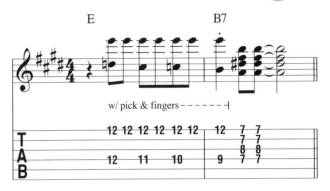

> **Swing/jazz Turnarounds**
> These two-bar phrases are often used as introductions and at the end of the eighth bar or 32nd bar of many songs from the '20s, '30s, and '40s, especially AABA-type songs.

➡ AABA songs are 32-bar songs that are divided into eight-bar phrases:

- An eight-bar section (A)
- The same eight-bar section repeated, but with different lyrics (A)
- An eight-bar *bridge* with a different melody, lyric, and chord progression (B)
- Another repetition of the A section, but with different lyrics

Here are some well-known AABA songs: "As Time Goes By," "Ain't Misbehavin'," "Georgia on My Mind," "Tiptoe Through the Tulips," and "What a Wonderful World." *All of these (and countless others) include the same two-bar turnaround at the end of the first and last A section:*

In the key of C, that's:

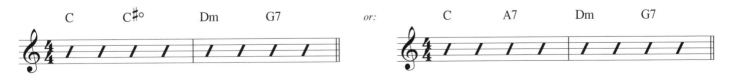

Practice playing this turnaround in different keys, like this:

Swing/Jazz Turnarounds

 42

Key of C:

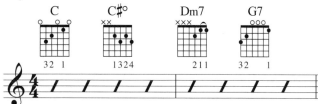

Key of G:

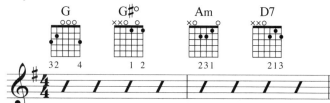

Moveable turnarounds

Key of G:

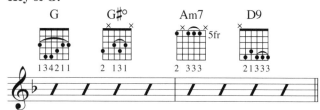

Key of B♭:

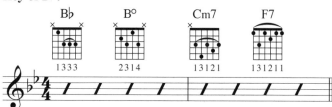

➡ The same turnaround is also used at the end of 32-bar songs that have this format:

- A 16-bar section is played
- The first eight bars are repeated but with different lyrics
- The last eight bars have a different melody, lyric, and chord progression

"All of Me," "Pennies from Heaven," "It Had to Be You," and "I Left My Heart in San Francisco" are all in this format. *The same turnarounds heard in Track 42 are often played at the end of these 32-bar tunes.*

➡ As mentioned previously, the same turnaround is often played as an introduction to tunes in both formats.

Summing up

These turnarounds enrich your playing in blues and in tunes from the "great American songbook." Also, now that you've heard and played many of them, you'll recognize similar ones when you hear them. You'll know how to play parts of countless tunes automatically; hence, another *shortcut*.

SHORTCUT #16: An Often-Used Eight-Bar Ending

Here's a way to automatically know the last eight bars of countless songs: The 32-bar tunes mentioned in Shortcut #15 that are not in the AABA format end with an eight-bar phrase that is "new information"—not a repeat of any other part of the tune. *In thousands of songs, this eight-bar phrase has the same chord pattern:*

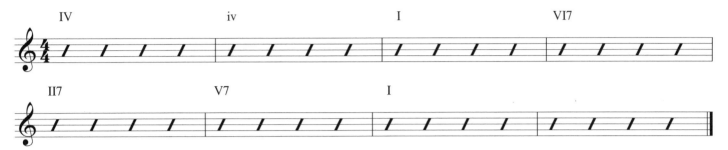

In the key of C, that's:

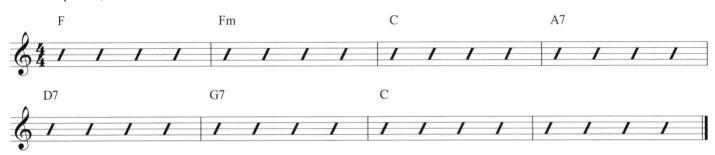

Often-Used Eight-Bar Ending

 43

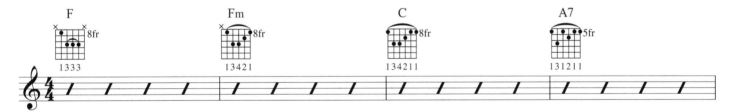

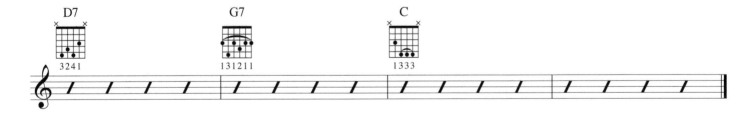

For examples, listen to "Pennies from Heaven," "All of Me," "I'm Gonna Sit Right Down and Write Myself a Letter," "Aways," "Paper Doll," "On a Slow Boat to China," "Who's Sorry Now," "Mona Lisa," "It's a Sin to Tell a Lie," "If I Could Be with You," "I Can't Give You Anything but Love," "Darktown Strutters' Ball," "At Long Last Love," "Slowpoke," "You'll Never Know," "Say It Isn't So," and "But Not for Me."

➡ There are slight variations from song to song. For example:

- The II7 can be ii.
- The iv can be #IV°.
- The third bar can be iii instead of I.

The old standard "My Melancholy Baby" contains the first two variations. Here are the last eight bars:

My Melancholy Baby (last eight bars)

 44

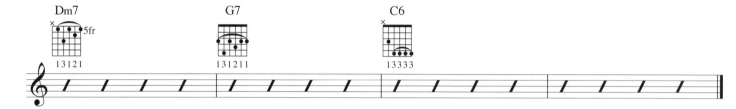

Summing Up

Listen to the songs mentioned above (on YouTube, iTunes, or your own collection) and try to play along with the eight-bar endings. Now you know the last eight bars to many old standards. That's usually 25 percent of the tune!

SHORTCUT #17: Three Often-Used Bridges

Most songs that have the AABA format have an eight-bar B section, usually called the *bridge*. In England, they call it the "middle eight." The bridge's melody and chords are completely different from those of the A section. Here's the shortcut: There are three "stock" bridges that are used in multiple songs. Once you learn these three chord progressions, you know 25 percent of a large body of tunes.

The "I Got Rhythm" Bridge (a.k.a. the "Sears Roebuck Bridge"): Named after the Gershwins' "I Got Rhythm," this eight-bar bridge is also heard in "Side by Side," "Straighten Up and Fly Right," "A Cottage for Sale," "I've Got the World on a String," "I Found a Million Dollar Baby," "Five Foot Two, Eyes of Blue," "Sunday," "What's the Reason I'm Not Pleasin' You," and "Please Don't Talk About Me When I'm Gone," as well as many jazz instrumentals, such as "Cotton Tail" and "Seven Come Eleven." If you are unfamiliar with old standards or jazz tunes, you've heard it in theme song to "The Flintstones." It goes like this:

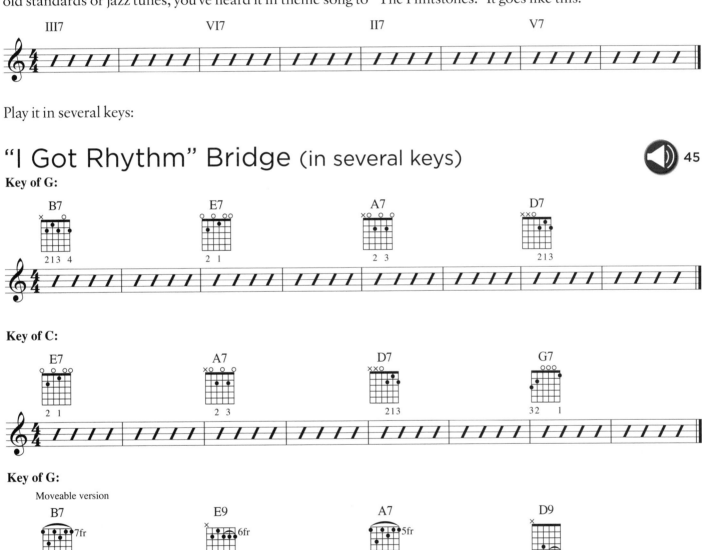

Play it in several keys:

"I Got Rhythm" Bridge (in several keys)

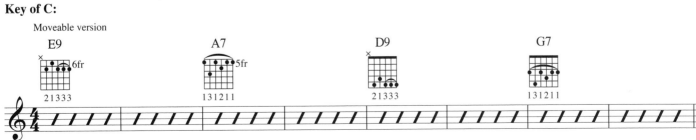

The "Honeysuckle Rose" Bridge (a.k.a. the "Montgomery Ward Bridge"): Named after Fats Waller's famous tune, this eight-bar bridge is heard in "Satin Doll," "On the Sunny Side of the Street," "I'm Confessing," "September in the Rain," "I Don't Want to Set the World on Fire," "You Belong to Me," "When You're Smiling," "Yes Sir, That's My Baby," "Nevertheless," "We'll Meet Again," "The Object of My Affection," and many more. Here it is:

Try it in different keys:

"Honeysuckle Rose" Bridge (in several keys)

46

Key of C:

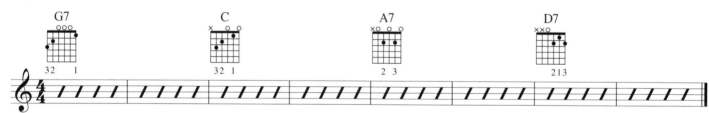

Key of G:

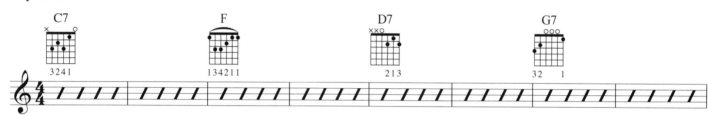

Key of C:

Moveable version

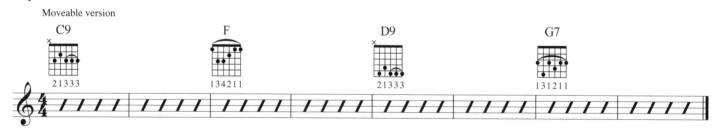

Key of G:

Moveable version

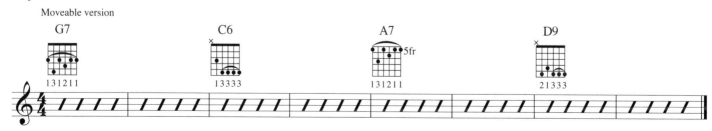

The "Happy Days" Bridge: Named after "Happy Days Are Here Again," it's also heard (with variations) in "Little White Lies," "More Than You Know," "No Strings," "Rosetta," "These Foolish Things," and many more:

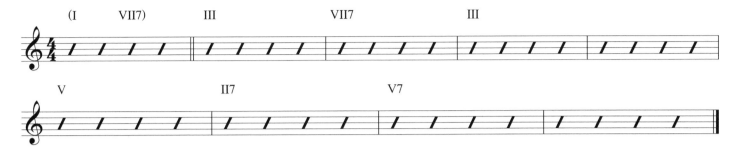

The I–VII7 bar is the last bar of the second A section; it "sets up" the bridge, which starts on the III chord. In the key of C, that's:

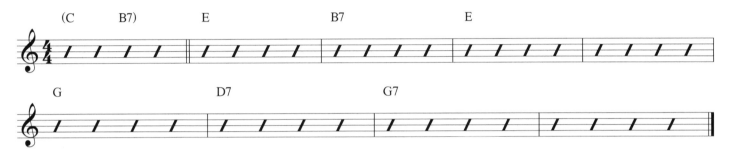

"Happy Days" Bridge

47

Key of C:

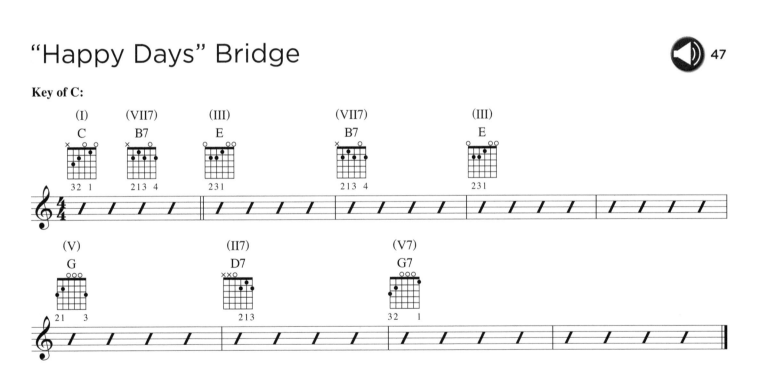

In this bridge, it feels like the III chord becomes the new key for four bars, then the V chord is the new key for the last four bars. The V7 chord leads back to I, because (as a future shortcut will point out) seventh chords usually "lead up a 4th."

➡ There are many variations of this bridge. In the most common variation (as in "These Foolish Things," "No Strings," and other tunes), the III chords are minor.

➡ In another variation, the fourth bar is a i chord. This happens in "More Than You Know" and "These Foolish Things."

Here's the interval formula for the "Happy Days" bridge with both of these variations, along with a sound clip:

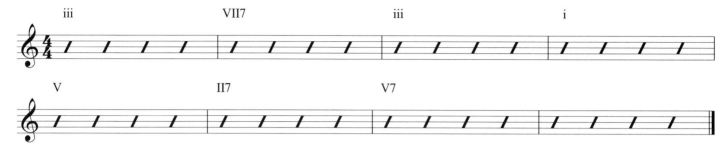

"Happy Days" Bridge (with variations)

 48

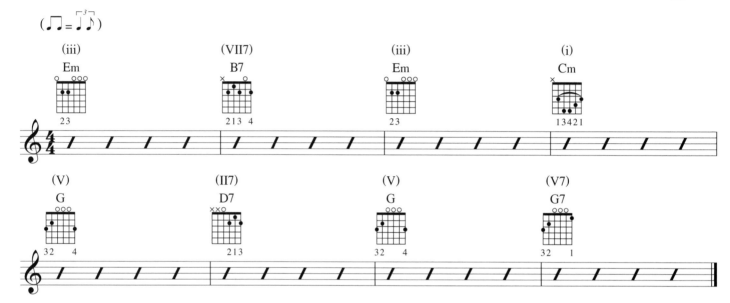

Summing Up

Once you're aware of these bridges, you'll recognize them when they occur, and you'll automatically know 25 percent of many AABA tunes. Hopefully, your ear will also become attuned to the many possible variations of these three patterns.

SHORTCUT #18: The "Rhythm Changes"

You've already encountered the "I Got Rhythm" bridge, named after the Gershwin tune. The A section of that tune is such a common progression that it has many nicknames: "rhythm changes," "ice cream changes," "dimestore progression" (this one needs an update for inflation), and so on.

It's the basis of countless standards, including (allowing for some variation) "Blue Moon," "Heart and Soul," "These Foolish Things," "I Got Rhythm," and "More," as well as doo-wop and classic rock tunes like "Oh Donna," "You Send Me," "Why Do Fools Fall In Love?," "Be My Baby," "Stand by Me," "Every Time You Go Away," "Every Breath You Take," "(Everybody Has a) Hungry Heart," and many more.

➡ In some tunes, "rhythm changes" make up most of the tune; in other songs, they account for part of the progression.

In their simplest form, rhythm changes are:

Examples include "You Send Me," "Blue Moon," and "Heart and Soul."

Stretched out (as in "Stand by Me" and "Every Breath You Take"), the changes look like this:

In the key of C, it sounds like this:

Rhythm Changes

49

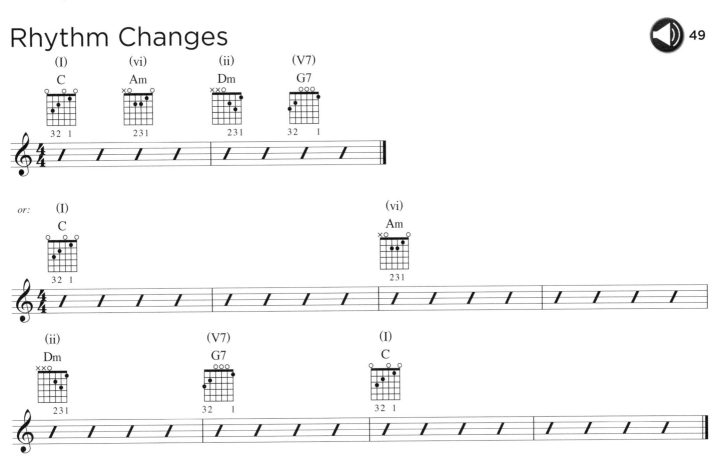

➡ One common variation: Sometimes the IV chord is played in place of the ii chord.

Practice the rhythm changes in many keys, using first position and moveable chords:

Rhythm Changes (in several keys)

50

Key of G:

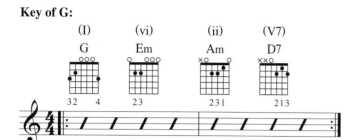

Key of D:

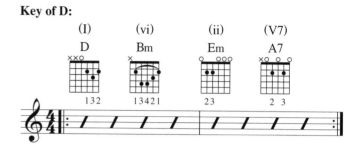

Key of G:

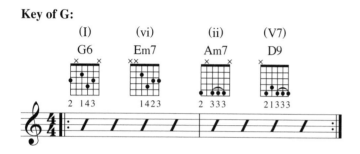

Key of C:

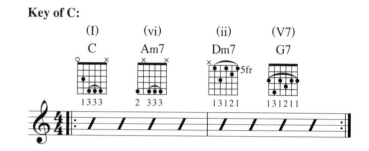

Summing Up
This progression occurs in so many tunes, knowing how to play it in many keys is an important shortcut to learning new songs!

SHORTCUT #19: Zig-Zag Progressions

This has nothing to do with cigarette rolling paper! In many chord progressions, you leave the immediate chord family, which creates musical tension. Then you resolve the tension by playing a series of chords that move up in 4ths. The "I Got Rhythm" bridge is an example, because it starts on the iii chord (which is not part of the I–IV–V chord family) and goes up a 4th to the VI chord, up another 4th to the II chord, up another 4th to the V chord, and, finally, up another 4th to the I chord. This is called "circle of 5ths" (or "circle of 4ths") chord movement, and it's explained further in Shortcut #24.

In countless popular songs, the chord progression consists (entirely or partly) of this type of movement. So, a shortcut to learning, playing, or memorizing this type of progression would be extremely helpful. There is such a shortcut *if you play moveable chords.*

When you play a circle-of-5ths-type progression with moveable chords, the sixth- and fifth-string roots of the chords (the bass notes of the chords) make a zig-zag pattern on the fretboard. For example, here's the "I Got Rhythm" bridge:

Four Zig-Zag Progressions

 51

Zig-Zag Root Pattern 1

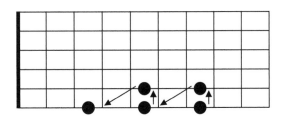

Key of G:

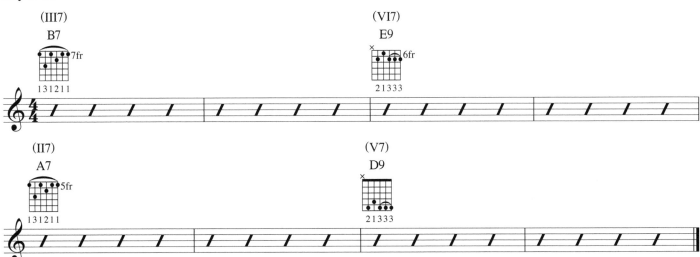

Some *circle-of-5ths* progressions are shorter:

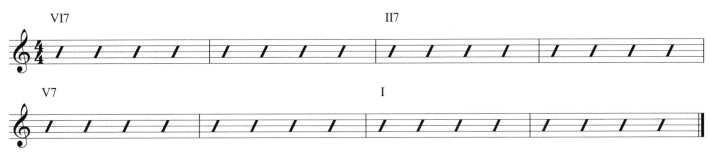

Zig-Zag Root Pattern 2

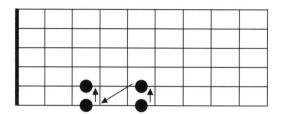

Key of C:

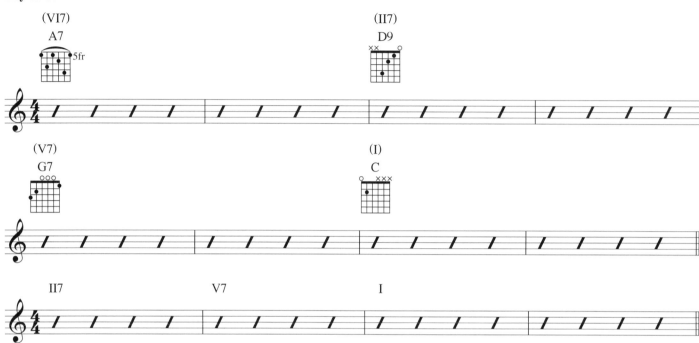

(VI7)   (II7)
A7   D9

(V7)   (I)
G7   C

II7   V7   I

Zig-Zag Root Pattern 3

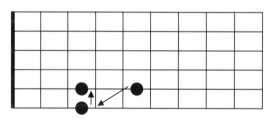

Key of C:

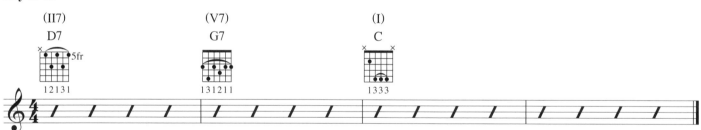

(II7)   (V7)   (I)
D7   G7   C
12131   131211   1333

Some are longer:

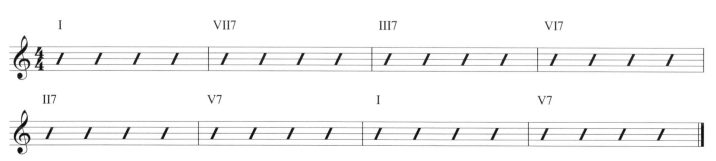

I   VII7   III7   VI7

II7   V7   I   V7

Zig-Zag Root Pattern 4

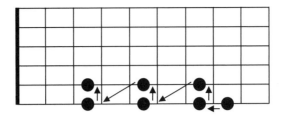

Key of C:

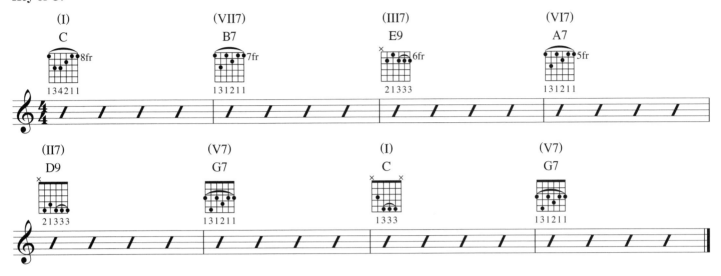

The above progression resembles the changes to the pop tune "Mr. Sandman." It starts on the I chord, jumps out of the C chord family to the VII chord (B7), and then goes up by 4ths until it gets back to C, followed by a turnaround chord (G7).

➡ The VII, III, VI, and II chords can be minor. All kinds of major or minor variations can occur, for example:

Whether the chords are major or minor, you're still going up by 4ths, and the zig-zag root pattern still happens.

➡ When learning a tune that has more than three or four chords, it may be helpful to play moveable chords, because the zig-zag root patterns are revealed.

Summing Up

Whenever a song has circle-of-5ths-type chord changes, you can use the zig-zag root pattern and automatically play a series of chords. All you have to do is listen and determine whether the chords along the circle are minors or sevenths (dominant), and then follow the root pattern.

MUSIC THEORY SHORTCUTS

Many guitar players are not interested in music theory; they just want to shred! However, some music theory is very practical. It can help your playing in a number of ways and save you a lot of time.

SHORTCUT #20: Octaves: A Shortcut to Learning the Notes on the Fretboard

You can learn all the notes up and down the fretboard by just memorizing the notes on two strings: the sixth (E) and the fifth (A). Octaves make it possible.

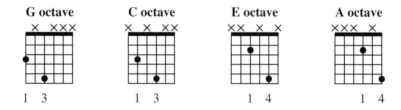

First, learn the notes on the sixth string. (Even if you don't want to memorize all the notes on the fretboard, you need to know the notes on the sixth and fifth strings in order to know where to place moveable barre chords or power chords.)

➡ Some people put temporary stickers on their guitar neck to help them remember the notes:

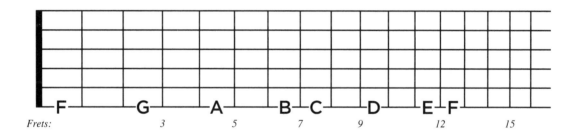

➡ The notes "between the letter names" are sharps and flats. *Sharp* means "one fret higher," and *flat* means "one fret lower." Each "in-between note" has two names. For instance:

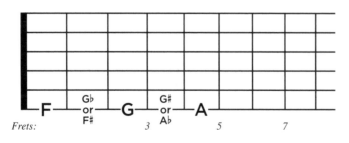

sharp = ♯
flat = ♭

→ Once you know the sixth-string notes, you also know the first-string notes because they're the same letter-names, though two octaves higher:

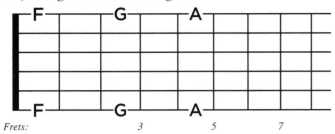

Frets: 3 5 7

→ Using octaves as your guide, you also know the fourth-string notes:

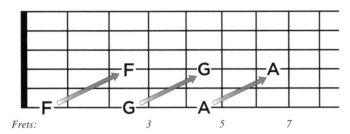

Frets: 3 5 7

→ Next, learn the notes on the fifth string; they're a 4th (four note names) above the sixth-string notes:

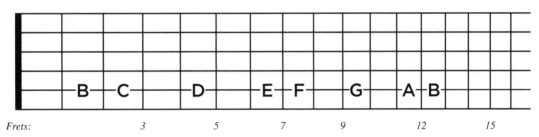

Frets: 3 5 7 9 12 15

→ Using the octave method, once you know the fifth-string notes, you also have the third string memorized:

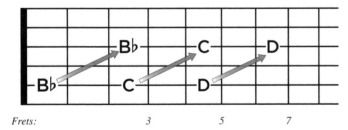

Frets: 3 5 7

→ That covers everything but the second string. Fortunately, another octave shape covers it:

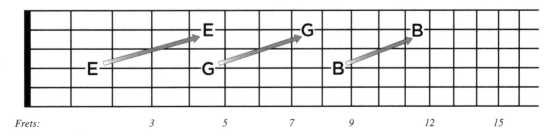

Frets: 3 5 7 9 12 15

Summing Up
Knowing the notes up and down the fretboard is helpful in many ways. Octaves shorten the learning process!

SHORTCUT #21: Finding the IV and V Chords

Intervals are the distances between notes. Intervals are numbered in reference to the major scale: going "up a 4th" means going to the fourth note of the major scale that acts as your starting point (e.g., from C to F or from E to A).

Musicians talk and think about chords and chord progressions in terms of intervals. Often, you'll hear "go to the four chord" or "go to the five chord," since these are such common chord changes. There are two easy shortcuts to help you automatically find the IV chord or IV chord. If you studied Shortcut #11, you already learned them:

→ If your starting note is on the sixth string, the fifth string at the same fret is a 4th higher. So, to answer the question—"What's a 4th above B♭?"—find B♭ on the sixth string (it's at the sixth fret), and the fifth string right under it, at the same fret, is a 4th higher. The fifth string, sixth fret is E♭, so E♭ is the IV chord in the key of B♭.

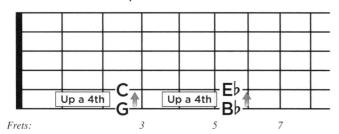
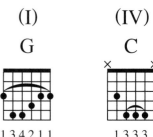

→ If your starting note is on the fifth string, the sixth string, same fret is a 5th higher. (Yes, it's a lower note, but it's the right interval—the fifth note in the major scale.)

So, to answer the question—"What's the V chord in the key of E♭?"—find E♭ on the fifth string, and the root of the V chord is right above it, on the sixth string—B♭.

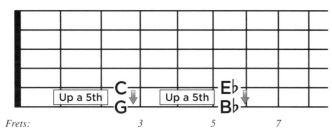
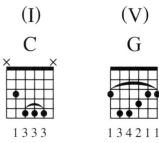

→ If you want to exercise a little more brain power, you could figure out other intervals on the fifth and sixth strings. For example, the III chord is one fret lower than the IV chord, in *any key*; so, if you can find the IV chord, you know where the III chord is located. All intervals could be worked out the same way.

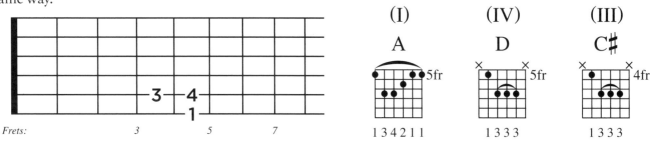

Summing Up
There's a very easy way to find the IV and V chords in any key, and you can stretch the concept to find other intervals, as well.

SHORTCUT #22: Simplifying Chords

There are basically three types of chords: major, minor, and dominant (sevenths). OK... four types if you count diminished chords. But what about all those complicated jazz chords like G13♭9, Am11, E7♯9, and C7♭9?

Almost all of the 5,679 chords in your *Chord Dictionary* are variations of the three basic chords: major, minor, and seventh chords. And, if you're reading a songbook and it challenges you with one of those complex chords (like G7♭9), you can simplify it and play a familiar, easy substitute. All you need to know is whether the fancier chord is a major, minor, or seventh variant.

Here's the shortcuts you need to know:

→ All the altered seventh chords (seventh chords with some extra note added) are still basically seventh chords. So, given G7♭9, G7♯9, G7sus4, or G7♭5, *you can just play* G7!

→ All the higher numbers (9ths, 11ths, and 13ths) are just fancier seventh chords. So, given G9, G9♯5, G9♭5, G13, G13♭9, or G11, *you can just play* G7!

→ All the altered minor chords are basically still minors. So, given Gm7, Gm6, Gm9, Gm11, or Gm7♭5, *you can just play* Gm!

→ Major chords have variations, too. Given Gmaj7, G6, Gadd9, Gsus4, or G6/9, *you can just play* G!

Of course, you lose some of the color or subtlety of the intended chord when you substitute a simpler chord. But it won't sound *wrong*; just not as fancy.

Summing Up

Once you know how to *read* the different chord types, you can simplify jazz chords and play easier versions of almost any tune.

SHORTCUT #23: Seventh Chords Lead up a 4th

Major chords have a sunny, complete sound; minor chords sound melancholy; and seventh chords sound bluesy—they have tension and seem to want to go somewhere. They do: they want to go up a 4th. Play a G7, then a C, and hear how the C chord resolves the tension of the G7. Do the same with E7 and A, C7 and F, and so on.

Here's the shortcut: when you hear a seventh chord, you know what the next chord will be. However, there are a few caveats:

➡ The resolving chord (the chord that's "up a 4th") can be major or minor.

➡ If the song is a blues, or a very bluesy rock, country or R&B tune, sevenths don't necessarily lead anywhere. This is the main exception to the rule.

If you've learned the notes on the sixth and fifth strings (see Shortcut #20), you automatically know which chord is "up a 4th" from any other chord because the fifth string is tuned a 4th higher than the sixth string (see Shortcut #21).

➡ Here's another useful fact: ninth, 11th, and 13th chords are just seventh chords with an extra note or two added, so they also lead up a 4th. E9 leads to A, C13 leads to F, and G11 leads to C.

Summing Up
Train your ear to recognize seventh chords. Then, when you hear one, you'll know which chord is coming next.

SHORTCUT #24: The Circle of 5ths: A Shortcut to Transposing—and More

THE CIRCLE OF 5ths

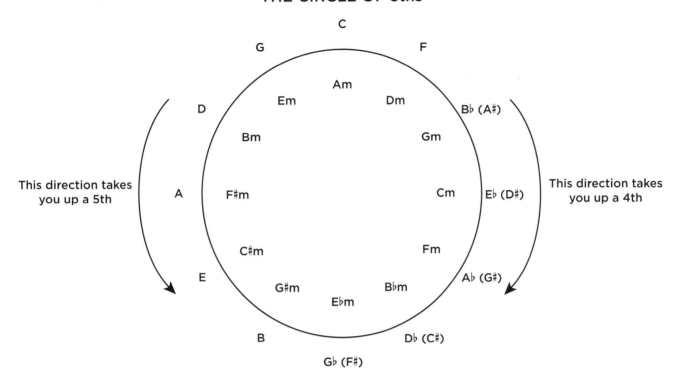

This famous diagram contains many shortcuts. It arranges all 12 tones (A, Bb, B, C, Db, D, Eb, E, F, Gb, G, and Ab) in a very handy order: when you go clockwise, you're going up a 4th, and when you're going counterclockwise, you're going up a 5th. F, one step clockwise of C, is a 4th above C; F is the IV chord in the key of C. G, one step counterclockwise of C, is a 5th above C; G is the V chord in the key of C.

➡ Sometimes the chart is written the opposite way: clockwise is up a 5th, counterclockwise is up a 4th. It only takes a second to see which version you're looking at (both versions are equally useful).

➡ The circle arranges chords in their chord families. Take any chord (C, for example), and its IV chord (F) is one step clockwise, while its V chord (G) is one step counterclockwise. The relative minors (Am, Dm, and Em) are next to their relative majors, *inside the circle*. **(First Shortcut: If you have a circle of 5ths to look at, you always know what the "extended chord family" chords are, in any key.)**

➡ But wait—there's more! As mentioned in several Shortcuts, many songs have chord progressions in which you leave the I chord and get back to it by going up in 4ths, or, as some musicians say, "going around the horn." This is depicted visually on the circle (go back to "Shortcut #19" and see how the "zig-zag" progressions all move along the circle, heading back toward the I chord). **Second Shortcut: You can "see" and better understand many common progressions by looking at the way they move along the circle.**

➡ Notice that, when you go two steps counterclockwise (e.g., from C to D), you're going to the II chord. Three steps counterclockwise (C to A) takes you to the VI chord. Four steps (C to E) takes you to the III chord. These intervals are the same in any key. For example, in the key of G, B (four steps counterclockwise) is the III chord. That's why musicians talk about II–V–I, VI–II–V–I, and III–VI–II–V–I progressions. These are all circle-of-5ths-type chord movements. (Yes, they are often described as circle-of-4ths movements, too.)

➡ If all of this is hopelessly confusing, here's a another shortcut that's easy to undersand: **Third Shortcut: You can use the circle of 5ths to transpose.** Transposing means changing a song's key. If you find a tune written out in a songbook in a difficult key, or a key that doesn't suit your voice, you can change it to any key by looking at the distance on the circle between the given key and your key. For example, if a tune is in E♭ and you want to play it in C: C is three counterclockwise steps away from E♭ on the circle, so to transpose from E♭ to C, you move every chord in the tune three counterclockwise steps: A♭ becomes F, Cm becomes Am, B♭ becomes G, etc.

Summing Up

You can use the circle of 5ths to find the chords of any extended chord family, to better understand many common chord progressions, and to transpose from any key to any other key.

SHORTCUT #25: Descending to the VI Chord

Many popular songs have a circle-of-5ths progression that goes like this:

or, in the key of C:

In other words, you jump from the I chord to the VI chord, and then go up by 4ths along the circle until you get back to the I chord. D7 is a 4th above A7; G7 is a 4th above D7; and C is a 4th above G7. (See Shortcut #24 for more on the circle of 5ths.)

This happens in bluegrass tunes like "Salty Dog Blues" and "Don't Let Your Deal Go Down," and in popular songs like "Lazy River," "Sweet Georgia Brown," and "Alice's Restaurant," as well as blues tunes like Robert Johnson's "They're Red Hot." Sometimes the I–VI–II–V–I progression constitutes the entire song. More often, however, it's a *part of* the song. For example, it's most of the eight-bar chord sequence described in Shortcut #16.

> **Here's the shortcut**
> Whenever you hear a series of chords descending from the I chord, one fret at a time, for four beats, it's a signal that you're hearing a I-VI-II-V-I progression. The VI, II, and V are seventh chords. Listen to Track 52 to hear how that descending series of chords sounds:

Descending to the VI Chord

 52

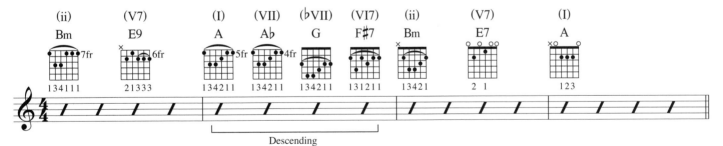

> ## Summing Up
> When you hear the descending chords described in this shortcut, you know what the next several chords will be.

SHORTCUT #26: BEADGCF ("Beadgucef"): A Mnemonic Device

A *mnemonic device* is any kind of word play that helps you memorize things, like "Spring forward, Fall back" or "Thirty Days Hath September…" "Beadgucef" (or, phonetically, "bead-juh-seff") might help you remember a good portion of the circle of 5ths. From B, going around the circle in 4ths results in: B, E, A, D, G, C, and F.

This is useful because in so many songs you go up by 4ths (e.g., in the "I Got Rhythm" bridge, explained in Shortcut #17). If you're playing a circle-of-5ths progression and land on a B, E, or A chord, "beadgucef" may help you remember how to go up by 4ths.

Summing Up
Anything that helps you memorize any part of the circle of 5ths will come in handy.

SHORTCUT #27: Finding the Relative Minor

Every major chord has a *relative minor,* a closely related chord that is a 6th higher. For example, A is the sixth note in the C major scale, so Am is the relative minor of C. If you play a C chord and an Am chord on the guitar (the easy, open-position chords), you'll see how similar they are. If you strum the C and the Am over and over in a rhythm, you'll recognize the familiar *sound* of the relative minor *in context.*

If a tune has more than just the immediate chord family (I, IV, and V), the next chords most likely to occur are the relative minors of I, IV, or V. In the key of C, for example, C, F, and G are the immediate chord family, and their relative minors (Am, Dm, and Em) make an extended chord family. A song in the key of C is likely to include one, two, or all three of these minor chords.

➡ That's why it's useful to know how to find the relative minor of any chord. Here's a shortcut that helps you do just that: *Go down three frets.*

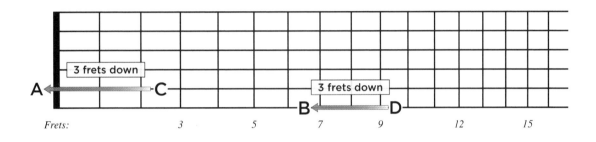

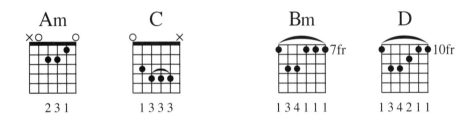

As the above figure shows, C major has a fifth-string root at the third fret. If you lower the fifth string three frets, you get the open A, so Am is the relative minor of C. What's the relative minor of D? There's a D note on the sixth string, tenth fret, so go down three frets to B. Bm is the relative minor of D.

Summing Up

Now you know how to find the relative minor of any major chord by using barre chords or open chords.

SHORTCUT #28: Figuring Out a Recorded Song's Key

Playing along with recordings is one of the best ways to practice and improve your playing. But you can't play along with a song until you can figure out what key it's in. Once you know the key, you can practice a scale-based soloing strategy or try to figure out the chords in the song and play along.

This shortcut helps you find a song's key by ear: *Listen for the ending chord.* Many people think the first chord of song identifies the key—sometimes it does, and sometimes it doesn't. But the *last* chord amost always does!

→ If a recording has a fadeout, so there's no clear ending chord, listen for the chord that *could* end the song; the chord that *resolves tension.* When you leave the I chord, you create tension. Coming back to the I chord resolves the tension. When you hear the chord that sounds like it could end the song, stop the recording and find that chord.

→ How do you find it? Play a moveable shape, like the F or D formation, and strum it while moving up one fret at a time until it matches the resolving chord.

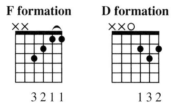

F formation

3 2 1 1

D formation

1 3 2

Summing Up
The resolving chord is the I chord.

SHORTCUT #29: The Capo

The capo (short for *capotasto*, the Italian word for the nut of a stringed instrument) is many guitar players' favorite shortcut. It clamps across the fretboard, raising the guitar's pitch. It's as if you paid someone to barre your guitar at a certain fret, leaving both of your hands free to play higher up the neck. If you know how to use it, it enables you to:

➡ Play in guitar-unfriendly keys, like B, B♭, or E♭, using simple, open-position chords.

➡ Raise the pitch of a song that is easy to play but too low for your voice.

➡ Play high up the neck (if you want a high-pitched sound) and still play easy, open-position chords.

Some people think using a capo is "cheating," but a list of famous players who have used one belies that prejudice. Muddy Waters, Doc Watson, Chet Atkins, Bo Diddley, Keith Richards, Ry Cooder, Robert Johnson, George Harrison, Eric Clapton, Lester Flatt, and Andres Segovia were all known to capo up from time to time.

Clamping a capo around the guitar neck raises the instrument's pitch. If you capo at the first fret and play an open-position E chord, it sounds like F. With the capo at the second fret, an open-position G chord sounds like A.

Moveable chords are not affected by the capo. If the capo is on the first fret, a barred G chord at the *actual* third fret is still a G chord. But a barred G chord *three frets above the capo* is G♯.

The following chart shows how to use the capo to play in any key. It offers choices for every key.

TO PLAY IN THE KEY OF:	CAPO AT FRET:	AND PLAY AN OPEN-POSITION:
A♭	1	G
	4	E
A	2	G
	5	E
B♭	1	A
	3	G
B	2	A
	4	G
C	3	A
	5	G
D♭	1	C
	4	A
D	2	C
	5	A
E♭	1	D
	3	C
E	2	D
	4	C
F	1	E
	3	D
	5	C
G♭	2	E
	4	D
	6	C
G	3	E
	7	C

Summing Up

You can use the chart on the previous page to place the capo where it needs to be:
- To help you play in difficult keys and still use easy chords
- To put a song in a key that better suits your voice
- To play high up the neck to get a different sound

ABOUT THE AUTHOR

Fred Sokolow is best-known as the author of over a 150 instructional and transcription books and DVDs for guitar, banjo, Dobro, mandolin, lap steel, and ukulele. Fred has long been a well-known West Coast multi-string performer and recording artist, particularly on the acoustic music scene. The diverse musical genres covered in his books and DVDs, along with several bluegrass, jazz, and rock CDs that he has released, demonstrate his mastery of many musical styles. Whether he's playing Delta bottleneck blues, bluegrass, or old-time banjo, '30s swing guitar or screaming rock solos, he does it with authenticity and passion.

Other instruction by Fred (and published by Hal Leonard Corporation) that can help you progress as a guitar player include:

- ➡ *Fretboard Roadmaps for Guitar, 2nd Edition* (book/CD)
- ➡ *Basic Blues for Guitar* (book/CD)
- ➡ *Fretboard Roadmaps for Guitar* (DVD)
- ➡ *Improvising Lead Guitar* (book/CD)
- ➡ *Dictionary of Strums and Picking Patterns* (book/CD)
- ➡ The Fretboard Roadmaps Series:
  - *Fretboard Roadmaps for Acoustic Guitar* (book/CD)
  - *Fretboard Roadmaps for Blues Guitar* (book/CD)
  - *Fretboard Roadmaps for Rock Guitar* (book/CD)
  - *Fretboard Roadmaps for Jazz Guitar* (book/CD)
  - *Fretboard Roadmaps for Country Guitar* (book/CD)
  - *Fretboard Roadmaps for Bluegrass Guitar* (book/CD)
  - *Fretboard Roadmaps for Slide Guitar* (book/CD)

Contact Fred with any questions about this book, or any of his other guitar titles, at: *Sokolowmusic.com.*

GUITAR NOTATION LEGEND

Guitar music can be notated three different ways: on a *musical staff*, in *tablature*, and in *rhythm slashes*.

RHYTHM SLASHES are written above the staff. Strum chords in the rhythm indicated. Use the chord diagrams found at the top of the first page of the transcription for the appropriate chord voicings. Round noteheads indicate single notes.

THE MUSICAL STAFF shows pitches and rhythms and is divided by bar lines into measures. Pitches are named after the first seven letters of the alphabet.

TABLATURE graphically represents the guitar fingerboard. Each horizontal line represents a string, and each number represents a fret.

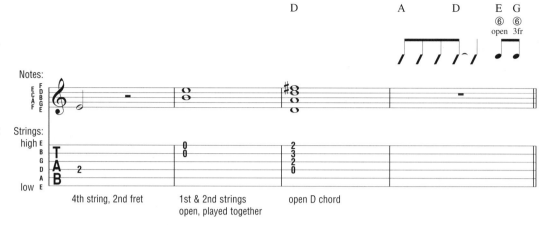

4th string, 2nd fret

1st & 2nd strings open, played together

open D chord

Definitions for Special Guitar Notation

HALF-STEP BEND: Strike the note and bend up 1/2 step.

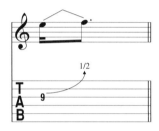

WHOLE-STEP BEND: Strike the note and bend up one step.

GRACE NOTE BEND: Strike the note and immediately bend up as indicated.

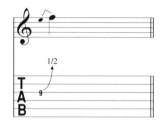

SLIGHT (MICROTONE) BEND: Strike the note and bend up 1/4 step.

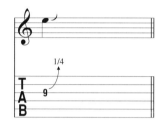

BEND AND RELEASE: Strike the note and bend up as indicated, then release back to the original note. Only the first note is struck.

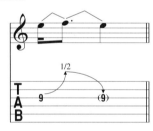

PRE-BEND: Bend the note as indicated, then strike it.

PRE-BEND AND RELEASE: Bend the note as indicated. Strike it and release the bend back to the original note.

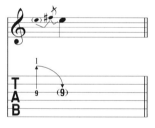

UNISON BEND: Strike the two notes simultaneously and bend the lower note up to the pitch of the higher.

VIBRATO: The string is vibrated by rapidly bending and releasing the note with the fretting hand.

WIDE VIBRATO: The pitch is varied to a greater degree by vibrating with the fretting hand.

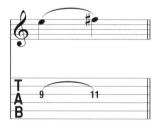

HAMMER-ON: Strike the first (lower) note with one finger, then sound the higher note (on the same string) with another finger by fretting it without picking.

PULL-OFF: Place both fingers on the notes to be sounded. Strike the first note and without picking, pull the finger off to sound the second (lower) note.

LEGATO SLIDE: Strike the first note and then slide the same fret-hand finger up or down to the second note. The second note is not struck.

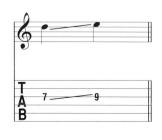

SHIFT SLIDE: Same as legato slide, except the second note is struck.

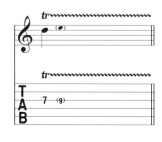

TRILL: Very rapidly alternate between the notes indicated by continuously hammering on and pulling off.

TAPPING: Hammer ("tap") the fret indicated with the pick-hand index or middle finger and pull off to the note fretted by the fret hand.

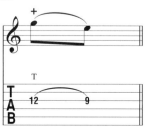

NATURAL HARMONIC: Strike the note while the fret-hand lightly touches the string directly over the fret indicated.

PINCH HARMONIC: The note is fretted normally and a harmonic is produced by adding the edge of the thumb or the tip of the index finger of the pick hand to the normal pick attack.

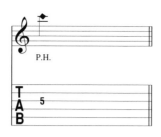

HARP HARMONIC: The note is fretted normally and a harmonic is produced by gently resting the pick hand's index finger directly above the indicated fret (in parentheses) while the pick hand's thumb or pick assists by plucking the appropriate string.

PICK SCRAPE: The edge of the pick is rubbed down (or up) the string, producing a scratchy sound.

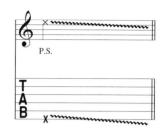

MUFFLED STRINGS: A percussive sound is produced by laying the fret hand across the string(s) without depressing, and striking them with the pick hand.

PALM MUTING: The note is partially muted by the pick hand lightly touching the string(s) just before the bridge.

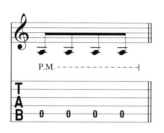

RAKE: Drag the pick across the strings indicated with a single motion.

TREMOLO PICKING: The note is picked as rapidly and continuously as possible.

ARPEGGIATE: Play the notes of the chord indicated by quickly rolling them from bottom to top.

VIBRATO BAR DIVE AND RETURN: The pitch of the note or chord is dropped a specified number of steps (in rhythm), then returned to the original pitch.

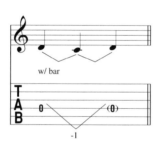

VIBRATO BAR SCOOP: Depress the bar just before striking the note, then quickly release the bar.

VIBRATO BAR DIP: Strike the note and then immediately drop a specified number of steps, then release back to the original pitch.

Additional Musical Definitions

 *(accent)* • Accentuate note (play it louder).

(accent) • Accentuate note with great intensity.

(staccato) • Play the note short.

 • Downstroke

V • Upstroke

D.S. al Coda • Go back to the sign (𝄋), then play until the measure marked "***To Coda***," then skip to the section labelled "**Coda**."

D.C. al Fine • Go back to the beginning of the song and play until the measure marked "***Fine***" (end).

Rhy. Fig. • Label used to recall a recurring accompaniment pattern (usually chordal).

Riff • Label used to recall composed, melodic lines (usually single notes) which recur.

Fill • Label used to identify a brief melodic figure which is to be inserted into the arrangement.

Rhy. Fill • A chordal version of a Fill.

tacet • Instrument is silent (drops out).

 • Repeat measures between signs.

 • When a repeated section has different endings, play the first ending only the first time and the second ending only the second time.

NOTE: Tablature numbers in parentheses mean:
  1. The note is being sustained over a system (note in standard notation is tied), or
  2. The note is sustained, but a new articulation (such as a hammer-on, pull-off, slide or vibrato) begins, or
  3. The note is a barely audible "ghost" note (note in standard notation is also in parentheses).

Get Better at Guitar

...with these Great Guitar Instruction Books from Hal Leonard!

101 GUITAR TIPS
STUFF ALL THE PROS KNOW AND USE
by Adam St. James
This book contains invaluable guidance on everything from scales and music theory to truss rod adjustments, proper recording studio set-ups, and much more. The book also features snippets of advice from some of the most celebrated guitarists and producers in the music business, including B.B. King, Steve Vai, Joe Satriani, Warren Haynes, Laurence Juber, Pete Anderson, Tom Dowd and others, culled from the author's hundreds of interviews.
00695737 Book/CD Pack...$16.95

AMAZING PHRASING
50 WAYS TO IMPROVE YOUR IMPROVISATIONAL SKILLS
by Tom Kolb
This book/CD pack explores all the main components necessary for crafting well-balanced rhythmic and melodic phrases. It also explains how these phrases are put together to form cohesive solos. Many styles are covered – rock, blues, jazz, fusion, country, Latin, funk and more – and all of the concepts are backed up with musical examples. The companion CD contains 89 demos for listening, and most tracks feature full-band backing.
00695583 Book/CD Pack...$19.95

BLUES YOU CAN USE – 2ND EDITION
by John Ganapes
This comprehensive source for learning blues guitar is designed to develop both your lead and rhythm playing. Includes: 21 complete solos • blues chords, progressions and riffs • turnarounds • movable scales and soloing techniques • string bending • utilizing the entire fingerboard • and more. This second edition now includes audio and video access online!
00142420 Book/Online Media...............................$19.99

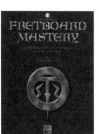

FRETBOARD MASTERY
by Troy Stetina
Untangle the mysterious regions of the guitar fretboard and unlock your potential. *Fretboard Mastery* familiarizes you with all the shapes you need to know by applying them in real musical examples, thereby reinforcing and reaffirming your newfound knowledge. The result is a much higher level of comprehension and retention.
00695331 Book/CD Pack...$19.99

FRETBOARD ROADMAPS – 2ND EDITION
ESSENTIAL GUITAR PATTERNS THAT ALL THE PROS KNOW AND USE
by Fred Sokolow
The updated edition of this bestseller features more songs, updated lessons, and a full audio CD! Learn to play lead and rhythm anywhere on the fretboard, in any key; play a variety of lead guitar styles; play chords and progressions anywhere on the fretboard; expand your chord vocabulary; and learn to think musically – the way the pros do.
00695941 Book/CD Pack..$14.95

GUITAR AEROBICS
A 52-WEEK, ONE-LICK-PER-DAY WORKOUT PROGRAM FOR DEVELOPING, IMPROVING & MAINTAINING GUITAR TECHNIQUE
by Troy Nelson
From the former editor of *Guitar One* magazine, here is a daily dose of vitamins to keep your chops fine tuned! Musical styles include rock, blues, jazz, metal, country, and funk. Techniques taught include alternate picking, arpeggios, sweep picking, string skipping, legato, string bending, and rhythm guitar. These exercises will increase speed, and improve dexterity and pick- and fret-hand accuracy. The accompanying CD includes all 365 workout licks plus play-along grooves in every style at eight different metronome settings.
00695946 Book/CD Pack..$19.99

GUITAR CLUES
OPERATION PENTATONIC
by Greg Koch
Join renowned guitar master Greg Koch as he clues you in to a wide variety of fun and valuable pentatonic scale applications. Whether you're new to improvising or have been doing it for a while, this book/CD pack will provide loads of delicious licks and tricks that you can use right away, from volume swells and chicken pickin' to intervallic and chordal ideas. The CD includes 65 demo and play-along tracks.
00695827 Book/CD Pack..$19.95

INTRODUCTION TO GUITAR TONE & EFFECTS
by David M. Brewster
This book/CD pack teaches the basics of guitar tones and effects, with audio examples on CD. Readers will learn about: overdrive, distortion and fuzz • using equalizers • modulation effects • reverb and delay • multi-effect processors • and more.
00695766 Book/CD Pack..$14.99

PICTURE CHORD ENCYCLOPEDIA
This comprehensive guitar chord resource for all playing styles and levels features five voicings of 44 chord qualities for all twelve keys – 2,640 chords in all! For each, there is a clearly illustrated chord frame, as well as *an actual photo* of the chord being played! Includes info on basic fingering principles, open chords and barre chords, partial chords and broken-set forms, and more.
00695224..$19.95

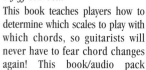

SCALE CHORD RELATIONSHIPS
by Michael Mueller & Jeff Schroedl
This book teaches players how to determine which scales to play with which chords, so guitarists will never have to fear chord changes again! This book/audio pack explains how to: recognize keys • analyze chord progressions • use the modes • play over nondiatonic harmony • use harmonic and melodic minor scales • use symmetrical scales such as chromatic, whole-tone and diminished scales • incorporate exotic scales such as Hungarian major and Gypsy minor • and much more!
00695563 Book/Online Audio $14.99

SPEED MECHANICS FOR LEAD GUITAR
Take your playing to the stratosphere with the most advanced lead book by this proven heavy metal author. *Speed Mechanics* is the ultimate technique book for developing the kind of speed and precision in today's explosive playing styles. Learn the fastest ways to achieve speed and control, secrets to make your practice time really count, and how to open your ears and make your musical ideas more solid and tangible. Packed with over 200 vicious exercises including Troy's scorching version of "Flight of the Bumblebee." Music and examples demonstrated on CD. 89-minute audio.
00699323 Book/CD Pack..$19.95

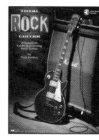

TOTAL ROCK GUITAR
A COMPLETE GUIDE TO LEARNING ROCK GUITAR
by Troy Stetina
This unique and comprehensive source for learning rock guitar is designed to develop both lead and rhythm playing. It covers: getting a tone that rocks • open chords, power chords and barre chords • riffs, scales and licks • string bending, strumming, palm muting, harmonics and alternate picking • all rock styles • and much more. The examples are in standard notation with chord grids and tab, and the CD includes full-band backing for all 22 songs.
00695246 Book/CD Pack..$19.99